GET INTO UX

A FOOLPROOF GUIDE TO GETTING YOUR FIRST USER EXPERIENCE JOB

VY ALECHNAVICIUS

Cover design: Jonas Perez Studio

Editors: H.P., D. Alsamsam, Robert Night Jr.

Illustration: Vy Alechnavicius, Illustrated with Miro using assets from Noun Project, Open Peeps

Kindle ASIN: B09GH7G2TN

Ebook ISBN: 978-1-3999-1026-2

Paperback ISBN: 978-1-3999-0771-2

For other versions, formats and reading experiences of this book please visit: https://bit.ly/GetIntoUX

Downloadable content: https://bit.ly/GetIntoUXContent

CONTENTS

For everyone who have been struggling to get into the competitive field of UX.

Special thanks to those whose questions, challenges and experiences informed this book. Without your courage to break into this field of complexities, kind words received along the way, and humility, this book would not exist.

"This is my portfolio, thank you for the feedback! I have been following your advice for a long time, and today I got an offer from <big tech org>, thank you for giving back to the design community"

"Hey Vy! I just got my first job offer as a UI/UX designer at an experimentation focused agency. Even though I don't really know you, I feel like you've been a pseudo mentor to me over the past year that I've been learning and forming my portfolio. I am super grateful for all that you've taught me and can't wait to finally work

"I just wanted to thank you for the videos you upload on youtube. I created a prototype which I shared with recruiters and was able to land a job. I hope you keep posting such wonderful videos and people get inspired to create something wonderful..."

"I am happy to tell you that I've received my first UX designer job offer today! You are a gem for people who have chosen the self learning route..."

"Just saw your video for 'UX mentorshop'. As always great insights! [...] Btw, your videos helped me get my first major UX job. I can hardly describe how valuable your content is, especially for people like me..."

"I just landed my first UX job and you were definitely very helpful, especially with the portfolio videos. Keep up the great work, I am sure many others will benefit from it!"

"Thank you for your videos, seriously! I'm a entry level junior and I'm looking for work right now, and you've made me realise I need to re-do my whole portfolio..."

"Just wanted to say that I've been following your work since I started studying UX. Finally got my first UX job thanks to your many tips on portfolio and interviews"

"Based on your videos I have been perfecting my portfolio, CV and interview questions/answers for the past month, I have just landed my first job in UX design! I probably wouldn't have even gotten to the interview stage without your portfolio and CV critiques..."

"Well thank you. Your information upped my game and changed my life. And it only took 3 weeks. That seems crazy to me. The offer I got was shocking. And I was completely honest with them about being self taught and wanting to learn more. So crazy..."

INTRODUCTION

Some years ago, I was working on my first degree in multimedia design and communication. The majority of the course work was influenced by user experience methods we know today. However, at that point, the term "user experience" was not yet widely used, though the industry was having conversations about better-quality, more usable web design. It was rare to find a professional UX designer.

The first time I read the definition of what user experience was, I knew I wanted to become a UX pro. What drew me in was the industry's understanding of user needs and its ability to challenge business assumptions. There were too many products and services that were poorly designed; rarely from a visual standpoint but rather in terms of usability.

Fast forward to today, and I've researched, designed and helped deliver hundreds of solutions. I've established and grown several high performing UX research and design teams. I pride myself on living, breathing and loving everything to do with delivering better user experiences.

As I developed into a professional, so did the experience design market as we know it. Today there aren't just UX designers but also UX researchers, content designers, UX engineers, copywriters, architects, unicorns, UX <insert a flavour of UX title>.

People assume this job rocks because of the immense industry growth, the demand for UX as a skillset, and our exposure to what great experiences look like. (It does rock.) They say things like: "I wish I could do what you do for money." Rightfully, it's almost like everyone these days wants to become a UX designer.

It's not just people. Businesses want user-centred design help too. Consider this conclusion of a recent study[1] from Mckinsey which evaluated **the actual business value of design: businesses that invest in their design capability outperform those that don't by double.** In other words, good design means a business can meet their bottom line, which means money.

The boom in demand for UX professionals can also be attributed to harsh competition in customer-first products and services. Businesses can't survive or gain traction without investing in their user experience.

Yet, if there's a sizeable demand for UX designers, why do so many of them struggle to find a job?

The high demand comes with a high entry bar. For example, you'll notice that junior positions in UX design and research require 1-3 years of commercial experience on average:

Junior UX Designer

- 1+ years commercial experience in UX design demonstrating an ability to clarify and communicate UX concepts

UX Designer (Junior)

- Minimum 1 years' experience working full time in a digital design role

UX/UI Designer

- 6 months to 1 Year of commercial digital product design experience.

UX/UI Designer

- Minimum of 3 years' experience in a transformational digital environment, telco experience is a bonus but not essential

Junior Product Designer (UX/UI)

- 2 years+ industry experience

Junior Service Designer

- 2+ years of commercial experience

In other words, in order to get an entry-level job in this field and gain experience, you must somehow already have experience. This situation is maddening to many entry-level designers but unsurprising to the experienced ones. Let me explain why.

The design industry has evolved over the years, and many designers have been giving back to the community (just like I'm writing this book to help you out). All the readily accessible learning material, online and intensive courses, bootcamps and certificate programmes are a testament that the times have drastically changed.

These days, I find aspiring UX professionals spend more time being confused about how to learn UX, instead of doing the valuable work of actually learning it and gaining experience. As a result, the market is saturated with people who know about UX but can't do proper UX research and design.

From the hiring manager perspective, nine out of ten candidates are not ready for the roles they apply for. They don't have real skill in the field.

Don't get discouraged, though. If you've learned to do UX properly and can show evidence of it, you will get the job without fuss, leaving those unqualified candidates behind.

Junior UX roles often ask for three years of experience but you can shorten this in half if you focus on the right things. **Imagine being able to demonstrate the same level of understanding and the same quality of work samples as someone who has three years of experience, but with less trial and error.**

Note that I won't give you an easy 'get-rich-quick' type of recipe to success in this book. You'll need to consistently show up, invest time, and grow into a UX designer or a researcher.

If you're willing to put in the right amount of effort, then this book will provide you with the appropriate tools, learning methods and a system to ensure that everything you do enhances your chances of getting your foot in the door of the industry.

When you're ready, flip the page and let's start.

---

1. The business value of design is a great report from 2018 (by McKinsey & Company) covering over 50,000 firms and their performance based on the design index: https://bit.ly/businessanddesign

WHY NEW DESIGNERS STRUGGLE TO GET INTO THE UX FIELD

The UX field has been booming for years now, and as a result, a landslide of new talent has flooded the market. All of the newcomers want to learn UX quickly, within weeks or months, and get a paid job. Only a fraction of them succeed. Why? Well, UX is too complex of a discipline to graduate into; it requires months and years of commitment to become good.

On the one hand, you have young designers struggling to find jobs, and on the other hand, managers who can't find enough experienced talent. I personally attribute this to gurus, bootcamps and other get-into-ux-quick schemes that overpromise, but never really make anyone fully market ready. If you're reading this book, you may be one of them.

While the new wave of UX designers struggle to get noticed, you have UX team managers who are virtually starved for qualified, confident and knowledgeable entry-level or junior designers.

I am one of those design team managers and today I am speaking to you, the newcomer who may not know where to begin. During my typical work week, I might review ten to twenty (sometimes more) candidates, and it's gutting when only a small fraction of them could be considered for the role.

I'll now walk you through the reasons why these candidates can't get in; I've observed these same issues over many years of hiring UX designers and researchers.

1. LACKING A FUNDAMENTAL UNDERSTANDING OF UX

Many designers tend to use experience design methods and frameworks on repeat without considering if such tools are appropriate in the context.

When reviewing entry-level portfolios, I see case studies that all use the same workflow and showcase the same artefacts: user interviews (often questionnaires), personas (often with elements that designers would never use to inform their work), empathy maps (that have no connection to anything else in the project), sitemaps, wireframes, mockups, etc.

UX stands for quality. It also means that to achieve quality, you will need to use different tools based on what's most appropriate and cost-effective. It's widespread to see juniors who use a set toolkit without understanding why those tools are needed or how the information captured would inform their next steps.

UX is deeper than a set of skills, it is a complex network of understanding, a combination of analytical and emotional intelligence, that feeds into this work.

2. MISTAKING UI FOR UX

Roughly nine out of ten junior UX portfolios I review focus on UI outcomes, patterns, branding and other glossy material. While these artefacts are part of the user experience design, they are not as important as the underlying user research.

When it comes to good UX, UI might be one of many ways to improve it, but it is not the only one, and it's not comparable to the full scope of UX. When working with junior designers, I constantly challenge them to consider if the UX work they are busy with could be done without adding a UI solution – the usual answer is no. That's precisely the issue.

In reality, UX is a process to deliver a better user experience. While designing experiences you might not even get to work on anything interactive, and that's OK!

The key is to apply proven methods to understand the users deeply, and then provide them with better ways to achieve their goals. That's not always accomplished through UI design.

3. LACKING COMMERCIAL EXPERIENCE

If you are hoping to gather enough commercial experience after you finish your course, studies, bootcamp, books, etc., you have started too late.

In practice, you should be freelancing, doing projects, spending every waking hour practising UX and ideally doing so for real businesses, their customers and users then capturing it all mercilessly. I will share more information later on about how you might do this without burning yourself out.

4. LISTENING TO YAY AND NAY-SAYERS

The industry is full of loud, highly opinionated UX specialists who have "made it" either too quickly or have been doing UX for a decade or more. They've become successful but also bitter and uninterested in new designers, methods and trends. As a result they are detached from the reality and struggles that the new generation of designers face when entering this competitive job market. They are the nay-sayers.

As gatekeepers, they have power over who gets their foot in the door in the industry, but their decisions are often extremely biased, making it difficult for newcomers to become successful.

On the other hand, you have the yay-sayers or, as I call them, false enablers. They are the inexperienced designers who evangelise and try to teach others the UX before they fully understand it or can caveat it end-to-end. They are giving advice when they, themselves, are not yet experienced enough to understand the field and its complexities.

Both parties are often out of touch. Ultimately, the contradictions and general noise distract juniors from becoming confident enough in what they know. It stunts progress and leads to unrealistic expectations and frustrations.

5. BEING TOO PICKY

UX is a career path that takes a lot of effort and time. These days, many learning providers promise instant job opportunities at big tech, "FANG" (Facebook, Apple, Netflix, Google), trendy startups and other companies with fantastic benefits. These are the companies that look killer on anyone's resume.

However, many of those great opportunities are location-dependent; they require years of demonstrable experience and can be counted on fingers... globally. Even if juniors aim for something less, the number of seats in established design cultures will always be limited, and those seats will mainly require experienced professionals.

Entry-level internships and graduate programmes are also too few to count on, and there's never a guarantee they will lead to extensions or permanent opportunities.

6. FOCUSING ON SHORT TERM OPPORTUNITIES

As I hinted before, user experience is not a discipline a person graduates into overnight. It takes time to be ready for it and even once you're ready, it could take years or decades to become proficient at most (and probably never all) UX skills.

This truth is often unsaid when junior designers are learning and trying to break into the field.

After finishing a course or bootcamp, it won't take long for a designer to realise that the market requires a deeper knowledge - there are simply too few openings to support a sudden influx of graduates and newcomers. Frustrated, they apply to every opening they can find and usually end up doing UI/UX or UI work, rather than truly user-centred UX.

Starting with UI is one of the common ways you can break into the field and then develop your skills, but it comes with a price. This one, and many other considerations, will be deconstructed throughout this book.

7. POOR PORTFOLIO CASE STUDIES

When I say 'poor portfolio case studies', I mean any of the following:

- Case studies unrelated to the prospective employer, their industry, complexity, design maturity, type of work and so on. For example, if all the cases in your portfolio are desktop UI/UX work, but the place you're applying for is a mobile app maker, then chances are you won't get in.
- Not telling a compelling story that engages and explains the work you've done to the hiring managers. I'll expand on this in chapter V: Demonstrate the evidence.
- Mistaking UI work for UX by focussing on the glossy outputs instead of the proper way to arrive at more meaningful outcomes.
- Displaying questionable work examples (such as illustrations, branding, video work, etc.). If you do so, make sure it's an obvious add-on, or better yet, put it in a blog post alongside actual UX case studies.
- Focusing on quantity over quality. These case studies have a lot of flashy, floating mockups but very little storytelling and substance that would showcase your understanding of UX, of the issue at hand, of the user needs, and other factors.
- Case studies that are either too general or made to impress your peer designers. Many entry level designers learn by copying the more established ones. What they often miss is the consideration of who is the target audience for the portfolio itself. For example, did you consider that your portfolio needs to speak to the hiring manager, not to other designers? Ironically, junior designers often forget to apply UX design methods to their own portfolios. This shows immediately!

8. LOOKING FOR A SILVER BULLET

Many designers-to-be are looking for the silver bullet when it comes to UX education.

I could bet that you picked up this book thinking that it would single-handedly open the doors into a UX career. That's only partially correct. You'll need to invest time in learning, practicing and collecting evidence to become hireable.

UX is an extensive field and a collection of a lot of complex skillsets that can only be developed through rounds of real-life exposure. Putting those skills into practice and solving real issues is what will grow your inner designer and do so exponentially.

Many designers opt for a single source of truth and expect excellent outcomes, but exposing yourself to many appropriate sources of knowledge will help you to become a pro sooner.

IN SUMMARY

Are you guilty of any of these mistakes?

If you can't recognise which of these issues are holding you back, you could seek feedback from more senior peers or UX design communities on social media. Ensure that you also ask for feedback throughout the process of applying for jobs and interviewing.

The idea here is to capture insights as though you were approaching a UX project, and to commit to remediate issues with appropriate actions. Addressing these mistakes can boost your chances of landing a UX job.

In the following few chapters, we'll dive deeper into exactly how to fix these mistakes.

∞

IS THIS BOOK FOR YOU?

This book is for you if you want to:

- **Set yourself apart** from the majority of entry and junior-level applicants by genuinely understanding what UX is and what it isn't. It's time to distil it into an effective workflow that adds clarity and pulls you out of the crowd of the unsure.
- **Set up your UX career for long term success**; learn the craft that is challenging, rewarding and future-proof.
- **Overcome the self-sabotaging actions** by focusing on the right things. Have you ever wondered why some UX designers get ahead quickly, while others take much longer? Hint: it's rarely to do with external factors.
- **Shorten your journey from beginner to pro** by using field-proven strategy and specific tactics. You'll learn how to go from awareness to 'can do' without getting stuck.
- **Ace your UX portfolio, resumes, and interviews** by showcasing your skills in the right way and for the right audiences. We'll unpack the essentials to get your foot in the door.

This book will not:

- **Make you a professional UX designer or user researcher**

overnight. You need to have a growth mindset, a passion for user-centricity and you should understand that this is a journey which will require unrelenting practice.

- **Improve your UI skills** or shorten the time you must put in to develop the technical design skills. If you want to learn a UI craft, reading a book is not the best place to start. Granted, I'll share some great resources that will help you develop those skills, but it won't be the primary focus of this book. Some UI skills can be acquired from books, such as technical and process skills like design systems or interaction principles. But that is not what I plan to cover. The best way I can recommend that you acquire UI skills is through inspiration from other great designers. As you grind through "pixel-pushing" repetitions (however harsh that sounds, it comes down to putting in long hours of experimentation with... pixels), eventually your UI and visual skills will improve, you'll develop your own sense, taste and style, and if it's what you're after, you'll become a master UI designer.
- **Be a single source of truth.** As a UX designer, and a "professional it-depends'er", you'll realise that there are many sources of truths. You'll need to explore many inputs until you can connect the dots and converge into a cohesive narrative for your users. It's the same with this book – it's another set of information signals that should validate what you already know, correct the rest, but more importantly, point you in the right direction and toward other actionable resources.

◇◇

HOW TO USE THIS BOOK TO GET
THE MOST OUT OF IT

To get the most out of this book, I'd strongly recommend reading it from cover to cover, even if you're a seasoned UX designer or researcher.

The first part of the book is very slow in its development, and the latter gains a sort of breakneck speed that makes it quite inconsistent. That's intended.

I wanted to ensure that we cover any and all gaps in your understanding before getting into actionable advice. As noted earlier, a lack of fundamental understanding of UX is one of the key issues keeping junior designers out, so it's important that you know where you stand as a designer and what skills you still need to develop.

The book is therefore split into 4 parts, each containing a handful of chapters with specific advice:

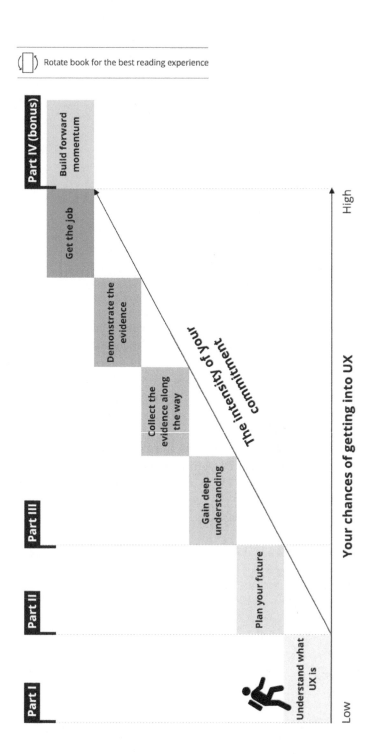

Rotate book for the best reading experience

Part I | Part II | Part III | Part IV (bonus)

Understand what UX is

Plan your future

Gain deep understanding

Collect the evidence along the way

Demonstrate the evidence

Get the job

Build forward momentum

The intensity of your commitment

Low — High

Your chances of getting into UX

I. WHERE YOU ARE

If in doubt, UX it. By that I mean, that you shouldn't follow your instinct to jump ahead and start working on any immediate fixes. Instead, as you would during the start of a typical UX project, I want you to go through this chapter with an exploratory discovery mindset. **Start with understanding what UX is and what it isn't.** This is crucial in order to align on what you should expect from a career in user-centered design and research.

This primer section sets the foundation for the transformational things to come.

II. WHERE YOU'RE GOING

Without knowing your end goal, how will you know what steps you need to take to progress? There are a lot of niches and industries within UX to choose from, and the journey to your ideal role may vary depending on which one you're interested in.

So in this part, I'll help you plan your career development. You'll **set a vision and an end goal** to ensure your long term success. Most importantly, you'll then define the smaller steps to that goal so that you can **start taking action now.**

III. HOW TO GET THERE

In order to land a UX job and arrive at your goals, you must **gain enough experience in UX.**

This starts with learning. You need to expose yourself to the appropriate material that will ensure you genuinely understand what the UX process is about, and more importantly how to do it. In this section you'll find handpicked learning resources, as well as advice on how best to approach them.

But passive learning is not enough. You need to apply the frameworks, methods and tools learned; practice your UX skills. Practice is essential to breaking into the field because the use cases you learn about in courses or bootcamps are far from real-world situations. As you practice your skills you will also gather evidence that you can do UX, which is what you need to get hired. Not sure where or how to practice? I'll share examples of how to find those opportunities and how to use them to boost your portfolio.

You'll soon understand why your portfolio (evidence) is the single most important thing that works as a testament to the strength of your UX skills and commercial experience. I'll also advise you on how to document the challenges, research, process and outcomes as evidence for your portfolio case studies.

With your portfolio sorted, the last major hurdle to getting hired is the application process which I'll break down in detail so you know what to expect. To succeed in this process you need to find the opportunities that are suitable for you, then market yourself and your capabilities correctly. I'll share specific advice on how to approach all of this so that you can nail your interviews and get hired.

IV. WHAT TO DO ONCE YOU GET THERE (THE BONUS PART)

What's next once you land that first ideal job? You continue to **build forward momentum in your career.** I'm including this section to help you focus on the right things to get ahead once you are in your first UX job.

This book is peppered with online resources and links to supporting materials. If anything I wrote or included raises your eyebrows, engage with it. Reflect and note it down. Don't just note the things that pleasantly surprise you but also anything you disagree with. You can learn from both examples, if not now then maybe later on as you get more experience and connect more dots.

As you will soon understand, learning does matter but it is what you do with what you've learnt that matters more. The secret sauce to getting a UX job is taking action. And on that note, let's get into it.

∞

PART 1

WHERE YOU ARE

CHAPTER 1

UNDERSTAND WHAT UX IS AND WHAT IT ISN'T

"If I had only one hour to solve a problem, I would spend up to two-thirds of that hour in attempting to define what the problem is.[1]*"*

UNKNOWN PROFESSOR AT YALE UNIVERSITY

Every entry-level, junior and sometimes even senior designer will make one particular mistake throughout their career. It's especially common among those who are transitioning into UX from related fields. That mistake is misunderstanding what user experience design is.

People with minimal experience, usually on the receiving end (e.g., tech-savvy people, customers and users), tend to mistake user experience for intuitive user interfaces.

While sometimes an intuitive UI is a good user experience, there is more to UX than just UI. In fact, most UX work is invisible and hard to define.

As a precaution and without boring you to death, I'll quickly run through the vital aspects of what makes UX so powerful. In just a few pages, you'll be able to distinguish what user experience is and what it is not. This information should then help form a strong baseline for you to continue further.

In the long run, understanding the fundamentals will also allow you to plough through the interviews and truly impress potential employers. How? You'll stand out from the crowd of designers who don't have a strong grasp on what UX is.

---

1. This quote is often credited to Albert Einstein in one or all of the following forms: "If I had only one hour to save the world, I would spend fifty-five minutes defining the problem, and only five minutes finding the solution." "If I had an hour to solve a problem, I'd spend 55 minutes thinking about the problem and 5 minutes thinking about solutions." "Given one hour to save the planet, I would spend 59 minutes understanding the problem and one minute resolving it." However, the earliest documented use of this quote dates back to 1966 when it was included in a collection of articles on manufacturing skills. The quote is attributed to an unknown professor at Yale University.

FIRSTLY, WHO IS A UX DESIGNER?

Let's start by unpacking the mysterious case of the UX designer:

- Who are they?
- What do they do?
- Why do they charge so much? (This is an actual question I've received from a product manager I worked with recently.)

There's no better way to get an answer to these questions than to get it from someone who has plenty of skin in the UX game. That's why I've taken the liberty to pull together a few different takes from well established, developing and up-and-coming designers out there.

Reading each of these tweets[1] will help form a broad, but also quite specific understanding of what it's like to be a UX designer:

A$AP Hockey @Tynell
Someone who makes a service/product/anything work AND look good. Everything is user experience.

Jason Mesut @jasonmesut
An evolved species of human that is either a) driven by passion to advance humanity, or b) earn lots of cash for moving boxes around screen and stealing practices from many established disciplines, or c) …

Richard Low @LWCARAB
They enable you to click or tap less to get the information you need! This in turn makes a happier user who then spends more time on the platform and spend more money so the company can pay the UX designer their huge salary.

Claire Durrant @claire_durrant_
1. "You know when a website or software pisses you off? Someone did my job badly."

2. "Understanding people well enough to design things that do what they need"

Per Axbom @axbom
A UX Designer listens to and mediates between stakeholders and affected parties, often using visual aids, to establish consensus and contribute to benevolent and sustainable products and services that promote well-being.

At least I wish this was true.

Chris Milne @ItsChrisMilne
Someone that builds something the way the people who will use it, want it to be built. Whether the user knows this or not. It's a collaboration of data and observations.

Mike Reed @mikereedwords
A person who makes (usually digital) products and services a pleasure to use

Jorik Elferink @JorikElferink
Making (digital) products easy to use and, ideally, addressing actual needs for people.

Nordic Oddchild @kaoticoddchild
People who translate the bad ideas from the corporate brainstorm into something wonderful that delights users.

Pause for a moment: which of these definitions resonates with you? Which definitions do you find surprising?

In my opinion, **a UX designer is the person who ensures that a product, service or any other offering (digital or otherwise) offers a great experience to its user.**

It almost doesn't matter what a UX designer does as long as they know who their users are and what challenges they face. A designer is able to take a simple brief with business goals, do a deep dive into their customers' lives to understand the current experience, outline where the opportunities are, produce meaningful ideas, connect the dots and work with other people to produce a better user experience.

Reflect on these definitions as they will help form the basis for your future self-development. They could also give you ideas for how you could market yourself to employers.

A REAL DAY-IN-THE-LIFE OF A UX DESIGNER

You might have seen those bootcamp promo videos with flying post-its, all-around high-fives, laughs and non-stop winning!

Perhaps you also have seen one of those YouTube videos titled "*A day in the life of a UX designer/product designer/user researcher*".

This is bubblegum content[2] that makes any experienced designer cringe. Why? It's a positive highlight reel showing people enjoying one work ritual or another. Often on their laptops, often doing only UI or product design, and even more often with minimal interaction with other people. I'm not even going to speak about the non-existent engagement with users or any other stakeholders.

The point is that what they're showing is not UX at all, and these videos only represent an aesthetic depiction, not a realistic description of a day in the life of an actual UX professional.

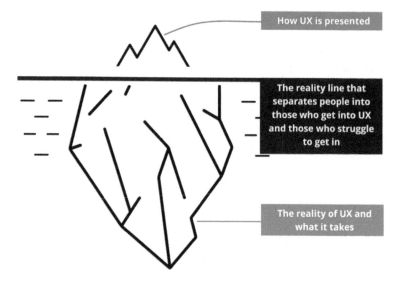

In reality, the user experience field is ultra-messy, challenging and far from the gloss and glamour of pushing fancy-looking pixels.

For example, on any given day, besides the activities you'd expect (as appropriate to the project lifecycle: user research, definition efforts, ideations, prototyping, validating etc.), a UX designer will be busy with:

- Team rituals (countless standups, retros and other agile scrum activities)
- Attending long meetings or meetings that could have been an email

- Dealing with organisational politics, which are always present to some extent
- Trying to dodge but more often than not actually dealing with a curveball of something not working out as expected
- Getting into proverbial wrestling matches with stakeholders, especially those who are difficult to work with
- Bringing the core team and stakeholders up to speed on the latest user research outcomes
- Constantly reminding the core team and stakeholders of actual user needs
- Fighting for the real user needs
- Deciding on appropriate steps for research and design activities
- Making critical decisions while facing plenty of unknowns
- Figuring out how to run enough research given the deadlines
- Evangelising (or brawling) about what UX is and is not, as well as the value it brings
- Balancing out stress and reward to prevent burnout
- Balancing out priorities
- Balancing out what needs to be done in the short, medium and long term
- Working on learning, achieving and progressing their career while doing day to day UX
- Working with often moving targets
- Managing change within the project and the organisation
- Making endless compromises

… And many more depending on the type, size, geographical location, culture and design maturity of the organisation.

To summarise all the above, **UX is more about change management and organisational adoption of user centric methods than about actual design**.

Ultimately, there are many critical factors that are omitted when selling UX to entry-level designers.

The typically glossy outcomes and extraordinary experiences are built on top of very complicated processes, juggling acts, compromises, and a tonne of people skills. Working with many people who might not be as much into UX as you are requires a full set of skills on its own.

The sooner you realise that learning a new framework, prototyping tool, or UI design technique is the easiest part of UX skills development, the faster you'll be able to shift focus to the bigger things that might be holding you back. What you need to do is to be ready to get your hands dirty again and again until it becomes second nature to use some of these harder skills.

---

1. The original Twitter thread by Jenny Theolin (Design director and strategist, @Jenny-Theolin): https://bit.ly/whatIsUXDesigner
2. Bubblegum content is how I describe content that is meant to entertain at the cost of truth or education. It's relatively easy to find examples of such content, but the point here is to avoid it. It lacks substance and won't help you grow as a designer.

UX IN A NUTSHELL

While there are many definitions of what UX is, there's one simple term I'd use to describe what a good user experience looks like: QUALITY.

Over the years of getting my hands dirty in product design, web development, user research methods, developing a business acumen and honing many other skills, I found that the key responsibility of any UX designer is to help facilitate the delivery of quality. **It's about designing the right things and designing them correctly.**

Firstly though, I want to address the UX vs UI debate. Misunderstanding this can affect your growth later down the line.

If you'd ask a stranger, or frankly, even someone from the tech world, what UX is, they will invariably describe UI. However, you, as a future UX designer, should be able to distinguish what is what. You should be able to showcase it in your portfolio and verbally articulate it as well. An inability to do so will block you from getting a UX job.

When I say that there is a crucial distinction here I mean that you need to be able to differentiate and communicate two things:

1. **UX as a result:** the optimal user experience for whoever the user is

2. **UX as a process**: an approach consisting of appropriate methods and activities to arrive at optimal user experiences

So, where does UI fit?

UI can be a vital part of both process and the result. The former being the act of designing interfaces for your user, and the latter stands for a ready-made interface your customers would interact with.

The simplest way to describe this is to say that UI design fits cosily within the UX process like so:

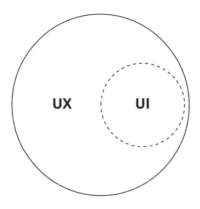

There's an awful amount of design memes online trying to explain this relationship between processes and outcomes. More often than not, they miss the point by being either too simplistic or way too elaborate so they end up comparing apples and oranges.

I've reviewed quite a few of these memes in the past in this short video: https://bit.ly/UXmemes. While the video is a bit tongue-in-cheek, it might help clarify these concepts for you if you're new to UX.

UX AS A PROCESS

You don't have to look deep to find frameworks for how experiences should be designed. My personal journey into UX started with Jesse James

Garreth's The Elements of User Experience[1] also referred to as the five planes of user experience:

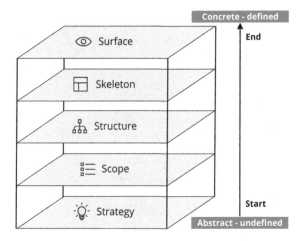

This is a great starter to define the optimal ingredients and layers of an outstanding user experience. You start with the abstract strategic steps and progress into the defined states with each new layer.

While the elements of user experience are a great starting structure, you will also need to understand the Double Diamond[2] model that the majority of professional UX and product designers today use to shape their work:

Rotate book for the best reading experience

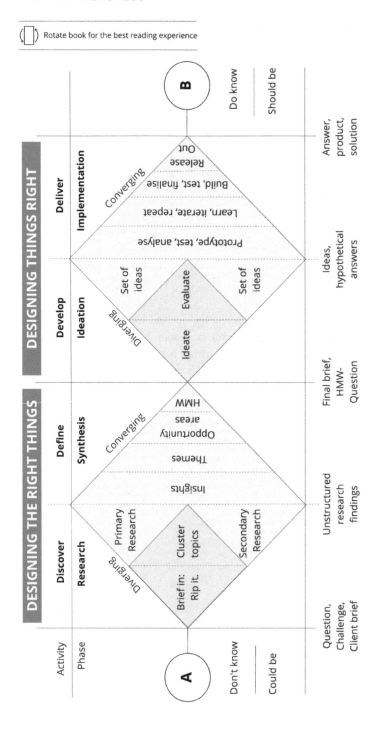

This model represents a holistic approach to designing quality services and products. It was created over a period of 17 years as several design leaders in the Design Council[3] worked together to outline the invisible design process.

The model is a foolproof introduction to UX for designers like yourself. That's how I look at it. By deconstructing the Double Diamond framework, you should be able to get a rough idea of how to handle any UX project. From discovering the right insights and themes, to ideating, prioritising and defining a solution.

Solving a UX problem, in a lot of ways, is making something out of nothing. You will have just the initial spark of a business problem, and from that vague idea, your job is to further define the problem, the opportunities, and appropriate solutions with the user in mind.

Not yet familiar with the Double Diamond framework?

Let's break it down.

∞

FROM A TO B

This model is so accurate to the UX process that you can't help but apply it (intentionally or not) as a UX researcher or designer. For example, in every project, you'll start at point A: don't know / could be, and end up at point B: do know / should be. It makes sense, right?

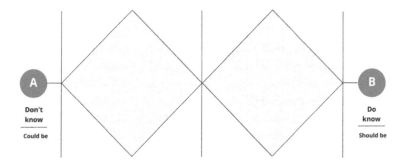

However, when I review many portfolios, designers and researchers new to this process sometimes jump into product design efforts way too early. Inexperienced designers tend to skip the most crucial parts: identifying and understanding the problem area, framing the problem, unpacking the user challenges and needs, and then finally moving onto the appropriate design efforts to address the well-researched challenges.

When designers do not adequately address these steps in their portfolio case studies, it becomes a weak portfolio because it does not demonstrate all of the activities and methods required at each step of the UX process (remember: it's designing the right things first and then designing things right).

As highlighted in the introduction, a poor portfolio is a key reason why an emerging UX professional may not be able to break into the UX field.

THE TWO DIAMONDS

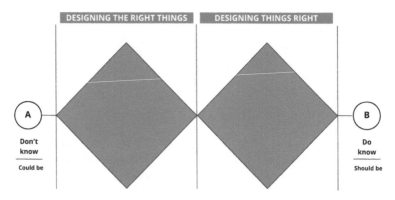

Looking at the image above, you'll spot a few brief messages:

- **Design the right thing**: This means using ample quantitative insights, but more importantly qualitative insights, gathered from user research to determine what you need to design.
- **Design things right**: This means that the process will include collaboration, compromise, and finding overlap between what the users desire, what the business needs to achieve in terms of viability and what's feasible technology-wise.

- **Design the right things + Design things right:** Quality user experiences.

PHASES AND ACTIVITIES

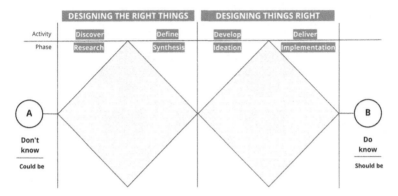

You'll notice that the segments inside each of the diamonds also represent activities and phases typical of the UX process. I'm sure you have heard of these before, even if the framework is completely new to you:

- **Discovery** - where you will run stakeholder workshops and user research activities
- **Definition** - where you will synthesise the research findings
- **Development** - where you will ideate, evaluate and prioritise what to deliver
- **Delivery** - where you will prototype your selected ideas, learn, iterate and hand the design over to engineering

Notice how I made some of the words above bold – in the industry, you'll find them used interchangeably. While terminology does vary, the sequence of the steps in a phased approach is always the same.

One of the last things that is worth drawing out on this model is the specific methods a researcher or designer like you could perform in the project scenarios:

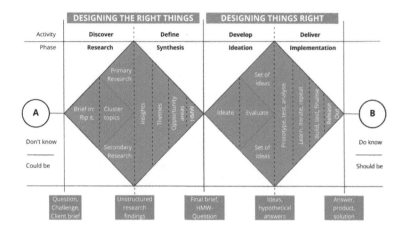

DIVERGENT AND CONVERGENT THINKING

Lastly, take a look at the Double Diamond diagram again:

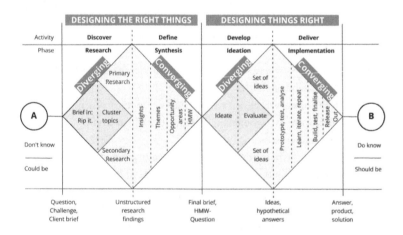

You'll notice that these diverging and converging funnels are the basis for the diamond shapes in this process. This is an essential part of the model that captures the unique thinking of UX designers.

Having a visual guide to outline how focused or open-ended you should be can make all the difference. For example, many new designers make the mistake of going to production way too soon because that's the easiest part to execute.

However, this is not the correct step to execute first, or at least not until you've outlined the optimal solution which considers the business, technology, and most importantly, user dependencies.

As a framework, the Double Diamond can tell you how broad your vision should be at any given point. It can help you decide when to branch your focus out, and when to laser in, converge and connect the dots.

Don't worry if you don't have a good handle on this yet. Reading about the model is a good first step, but practice is what will solidify it in your mind.

If you'd like more information about how to use the Double Diamond or about convergent and divergent thinking in practice, you can head over to my YouTube channel: https:// bit.ly/DDexplained.

At a minimum, I suggest that you deconstruct, learn and memorise this model. The amount of junior, mid- and senior-level designers I've interviewed who cannot briefly describe their UX process is alarming.

Frameworks like this one show that you know what UX is and they help you communicate your design process in a concise and clear way, which matters especially when you're presenting your project examples to someone from outside the field.

FULL SET OF UX DISCIPLINES, BEST PRACTICES AND OTHER ESSENTIAL TOOLS

During the UX process, you must employ appropriate principles and guidelines to stay impartial when solving problems for other people.

Commonly, designers err by designing solutions for themselves. They might think that mere empathy (more often than not by proxy i.e. without engaging with actual users) is enough to understand what the user issues are and jump straight into ideations, prototyping and testing.

To avoid this, you must familiarise yourself with the right toolkit to help you make unbiased, informed, and justified decisions throughout the design process.

The toolkit I'd like to share with you includes:

UX psychology, human factors and cognitive biases

Even if you don't plan to specialise in UX research, understanding human factors that influence attitudes and behaviours is the bedrock of designing user experiences.

There are hundreds of behavioural studies, documented cognitive biases and many other proven universal factors that you should know about. After all, your solutions must cater to the drivers and motivations in our day-to-day lives.

You need to know just enough to understand the user deeply, rather than attributing empathy from your own experiences to the end-user. This is how you add value for both the customer (usually, the business) and for the end-user of your solutions.

Usability best practices and heuristics

Between 1990-1994, Jacob Nielsen came up with one of the most influential lists of heuristics for interactive product and UI usability. It almost doesn't matter what book on UX you pick up, some version of Nielsen's list will be used.

It's a good idea to learn these principles by heart so that when you do a heuristic evaluation of the current experience to inform your work, you can make sound decisions that result in intuitive interactions.

Information architecture (IA)

This original definition of user experience is about three simple things: context, content and the user. When deciding how to present information in your UX process you must consider who this information is for and in what context it must be shown. This will then inform your efforts to outline how it should be presented.

While I make it sound simple, IA is a very complex part of the user experience design process. In particular, it can be challenging when you must sort out complex or big-data-based issues. Information architecture should be one of the first areas to look into as you develop your skills.

The UX commandments
Stemming from the points above, there is a selection of super-specific commandments and proven guidelines coined by various psychologists, researcher fellows, usability experts and design leaders. These commandments include the better-known Gestalt laws, Miller's and Fitz' laws but there's more.

Accessibility
It's crucial to look into designing inclusive and accessible solutions from day one as a UX researcher or designer. Many juniors tend to overlook accessibility because it requires extra time and effort to cater to what seems like a minority audience. But this is typical of business thinking, not of UX. Designing an experience for the minority means designing for all of your users.

When creating a tool for factory workers, for example, you should always make a solution more usable under various conditions. To do so, you must address all challenges, from situational (e.g. loud environment), to temporary (e.g. ear infection), to permanent (e.g. deafness), so you can make it work for everyone, regardless of disabilities or temporary setbacks.

It is not just the right thing to do; it will make your design solutions work consistently. As before, make sure to always dig deep.

Humane design and ethics
While ethics and moral codes aren't universal (think of the differences between cultures or sides of the globe), human values are[4]. Understanding what they are and fighting for fairer experiences is a big part of all human centred jobs (UX included).

It's common for organisations to lose the care for people and humanity, once they reach a point of expansion where they no longer have skin in the game. However, you as a UX designer can still make a difference.

Questioning the business intent, weighing different options, having challenging conversations and taking a stance are just some of the ways to ensure that as you design new products into life, you don't end up creating the next atomic bomb[5].

All other disciplines
Aside from a few handpicked disciplines, a growing UX designer or researcher should explore and hone skills from outside UX as well. You might have seen a variation of this map before that unpacks user experience design in all of its glory:

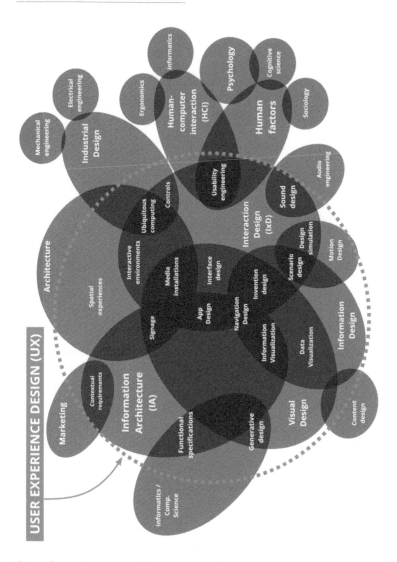

This infographic, adapted from Dan Saffer's original map[6] of UX disciplines, is a visual representation of why it takes years to become proficient in UX.

The only thing that is missing in this map is also the most important part of UX: user research. **To deliver an outstanding user experience, you must do UX research on every project regardless of the disciplines involved.** Without it, your solutions might be usable and look good but they won't land with the intended audience as expected.

In the next chapter I'll explain further why UX research matters so much. I'll also highlight some of the best resources to help you build a foundation for doing good UX work.

∞

1. *The Elements of User Experience* is a timeless book containing by far the easiest-to-grasp definition of user experience design. You should definitely put it on your reading list.
2. "Eleven lessons. A study of the design process" (PDF). Design Council. Retrieved 6 April 2021.
3. Established in Winston Churchill's 1944 wartime government as the Council of Industrial design (COID). It was created to promote economic recovery through applied design standards in British products.
4. An interesting study taking a look at human factors and values in particular is *Value hierarchies across cultures*, Shalom H.Schwartz, Anat Bardi, 2001: https://bit.ly/valuehierarchies. See more in the bibliography at the end of this book.
5. Sometimes the drive to innovate and the novelty of tech cause people to overlook bad outcomes. Here I want to use the example of J. R. Oppenheimer who created the "destroyer of worlds" - the first atomic bomb. After the first successful detonation of his bomb in 1945 Oppenheimer used Hindu scriptures to describe the outcomes of his design: *"Now I am become Death, the destroyer of worlds.*
6. In 2008 Product design leader Dan Saffer mapped out the various disciplines that feed into UX to highlight how vast the world of user experience design really is.

THERE IS NO UX WITHOUT USER RESEARCH

Users will have experiences regardless of whether you run proper user research. You can design any experience without deeper insights. You can also ideate on it and quickly produce products or services. Yet, the quality of the experience won't be as excellent as it could have been had your process included research.

One of the most important things about UX is that THERE IS NO UX DESIGN WITHOUT USER RESEARCH.

Don't gloss over it - this is a critical paradigm that, if ignored, can stunt your development or make you unhireable. Ignoring user research or doing it at a subpar quality will water down the strength of your UX case studies, and as a result, your job application.

As a UX team manager and a hiring manager myself, the first thing I look for in potential candidates is whether they know what UX is about. I want to see that they have user centricity which can only be achieved through user research.

It's common to see designers who have fantastic product or UI design skills but still can't break into the professional UX world. They often lack the one thing that makes UX designers so effective: a thorough user research approach.

A colleague of mine once quoted his design teacher as having described one approach to UX as: *"Research a lot, design little"*[1]. I love this and agree with the teacher completely. In fact, I bring this very slogan into my entire philosophy for leading design strategy and teams. These few words really capture what professional UX designers do and what they don't do.

∞

THE UX RESEARCH APPROACH IN A NUTSHELL

Often new designers make a mistake by researching an area once and then defaulting to product design or UI efforts without running continuous user research for the specific scenarios and segments of the projects they work on. Needless to say, this shows in portfolios and also comes out in interviews, as you'll always be asked about it.

User research should be run in a continuous cumulative fashion where the project team goes through discovery, design, and delivery cycles. This is because to UX things properly, you must understand each case in depth.

For example, all the natural, as-is, day-to-day experiences of our users must be understood for each project because the target audience may be different. You can take this profile of the audience to identify and outline the suitable journeys, steps, pain points, why they do the things they do, and the tremendous challenges they face—all of the things that you and your team can translate into opportunities for improvement.

When working with a team on a project or initiative, you'll need to go through several steps: from planning to execution to distilling the insights that can become actionable.

For simplicity's sake, I usually break any research effort into the following six steps:

1. **Frame the problem**: Outline the problem area to target.
2. **Define the hypotheses**: Based on the evidence accumulated to date, identify what the potential opportunity areas to improve user experience are.
3. **Plan the research**: Cover the consideration, gaps, and possible targeting methods.
4. **Conduct the research**: Run the research effort.
5. **Synthesise the research**: Review, map, and assess the findings.
6. **Share and action**: Play back the findings, themes, and insights to inform the next steps.

THE THINGS YOU NEED TO CONSIDER

When it comes to planning user research methods, the following are critical themes and questions to consider:

- **Goals:** Always identify the goal of the project before diving in. Why does the business need a user-centric approach and the deep insights that only user research can uncover?
- **Evidence:** Given the grand goals that the business has, what is presumed right now? What evidence do stakeholders have? What are the high-level hypotheses that can inform your research plan? What sounds right and what does not? Take anything the business states as a given with a massive spoonful of salt as businesses are rarely right about their customers or users – that's precisely why they need your UX help.
- **Cost & timeframe:** While you want to research the product or service space continuously and endlessly, you often need to determine the minimum amount of research needed to inform the next steps due to costs and timeframes. While time and cost awareness deserves its own book, I usually advise juniors to work backwards from the goals and outcomes in order to pick the appropriate methods, activities and otherwise set pace for the research effort.
- **Users:** Target the right audience involved in the current experience and outline who the new user experience will be for. Consider who the users are and how you will find them— you wouldn't want to design without research or to do the research on the wrong subjects. The availability of said users –

admin and planning to get access to them – can be time-consuming so it's important that it's not overlooked.

- **People behaviours vs attitudes:** the division here does not mean that you must pick one or the other. You need to cover both. Business stakeholders usually have some notion of their users' attitudes and only a hunch about their real-life behaviours.

- **Quant vs qual:** as with the previous point, the "vs" represents division, not a choice between the two. A lot of designers start with quant and follow up with qual. In practice, that's a good enough general approach for beginners. Still, as you grow into authentic UX specialist shoes, you'll need to be able to both drive with quantitative measures (where necessary), as well as do research for qualitative insights to truly understand the depth of issues.

The two final points above are the most significant. These are what's commonly labelled as the four dimensions for picking the right user research tools:

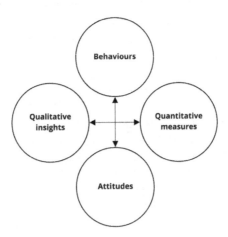

Your research will always focus on discovering what the users say (user attitudes) and what the users do (behaviours), and then expressing that in quantitative measures (indirect insights: what, where, how many), and qualitative insights (direct insights: who, what, how and, most importantly, why).

∞

THE ESSENTIAL UX RESEARCH METHODS

If you look around, you will not find an easy-to-follow UX research checklist. This is because every problem requires appropriate methods, and often a complex, multi-faceted approach that will yield valuable insights in the most cost-effective way.

Even if there was a checklist or a set of rules, a textbook would not be the best medium for learning them. Instead you should first consider the research principles that are shared by different UX pros, even when their approaches and methods differ. These principles, which I'll outline next, take a scientific approach to research efforts.

Learn them, then practice them in a safe environment, for example as part of conceptual and side projects, shadowing and apprenticeship opportunities. If you are able to work with a good mentor, or someone with a few more years of experience, this will vastly boost your ability to learn how to choose between different methods[2].

Rotate book for the best reading experience

What do you need to research and how should you approach it?

○ Natural use   △ Scripted use   ◇ De-contextualised / no usage   ☆ Combined / hybrid

Behavioural
(what they do)

Attitudinal
(what they say)

Qualitative (direct)

Quantitative (indirect)

- ▲● Eye tracking
- ▲ Usability benchmarking (lab)
- ▲ Moderated remote usability studies
- ▲ Unmoderated remote panel studies
- ● Clickstream analysis
- ● A/B testing
- ▲ Unmoderated UX studies
- ● True intent studies

- ▲ Usability studies (lab)
- ● Ethnographic field studies

- ◆ Concept testing
- ● Diary studies
- ● Customer feedback
- ◆ Desirability studies
- ★ Card sorting

- ● Intercept surveys
- ★ Email surveys

- ◆ Participatory design
- ★ Focus group
- ★ Interviews

- **Natural use:** observing and capturing how users use a product without interruptions or guidance by the researcher. The simplest way to think about these methods is that they're allowing the user to provide feedback without asking them for it. Users can be observed in their most natural state without compromising the insights.
- **Scripted use:** a targeted and guided approach to capturing how users would use a product or service. This is often done in remote or lab scenarios to capture additional feedback that's required to validate ideas.
- **De-contextualised / no usage:** I like to describe these methods as social product or service shaping activities. For example, participatory design is a great way to involve users and other stakeholders in the design process to ensure that all the happy and the unhappy paths[3] are captured. Desirability studies and concept testing allows teams to validate their ideas quickly, and gauge the potential outcomes of introducing certain features.
- **Combined / hybrid:** methods that require to merge several different ways in order to capture enough insights. For example, during the interview process you might outline high-level ethnographic insights, gauge desirability, capture customer feedback, etc. This is also the key reason so many designers and researchers tend to default to interviews, as they can cover a lot of ground. However, make sure to reflect if that is enough to inform yours and your team's next steps. Often you'd still require deeper dives that can only be supported by appropriate natural use, scripted and de-contextualised methods.

---

1. *"Research a lot, design little"* - I first heard this powerful quote from colleague and talented experience designer Dan Holder. It's one worth keeping in mind when doing UX.
2. This matrix of UX research methods is based on NNG / Chris Roher's Landscape of UX research methods. To dive deeper into the latter, visit: https://bit.ly/UXRmethods
3. Happy paths are user journeys that outline the ideal steps users would take to fulfil their tasks without issues. Unhappy paths cover the exceptions, errors, unexpected issues in your product. For example, a happy path for a user could be to buy postage stamps

using an online app, and unhappy path in this case might be the steps user would have to take if they couldn't access the app (no internet or the servers are down) so they have to go to the post office or use an alternative service to buy stamps. Another example is if they needed a special stamp that they can't purchase through your app. It is important for UX designers to focus on the unhappy paths as much as the happy ones.

EXAMPLE ILLUSTRATIVE CASE

Let's say that you are brought in to redesign an existing web app used by employees of a large organisation. This app is not a public tool as hundreds of the organisation's own lab technicians are meant to use it to log every decision they make in their day-to-day work. Unfortunately, many don't.

The business goal is to improve the app usage so that the decision-making process is logged more effectively.

A product manager has used the Google Analytics tracking in the web app to identify the areas that could use improvement. Their hypothesis is that the reason users don't engage with the app proactively is because it has poor usability and looks dated.

First and foremost you should try to frame the problem here:

- Why does the business need to improve the engagement with the app?
- Why now?
- How does it connect to their bottom line (profit increase, cost reduction)?
- Why do the targeted employees (lab technicians) not use the app in their day-to-day scenarios?

- What is the business missing right now, and what opportunities have they identified so far?
- Who are the key users, and what attitudes and behaviours have business stakeholders captured so far?
- What are the high level hypotheses?

By answering these and other questions through stakeholder interviews and workshops, you'll develop a good enough hypothesis(es) to engage in further, mixed methods user research.

EXAMPLE RESEARCH STEPS

To help you better wrap your head around the consideration factors described above, here's how an oversimplified user research approach could look like for this case:

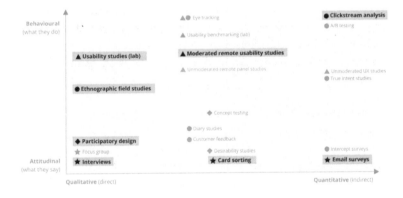

Extracting the key activities and putting them into a more linear flow would result in a plan like this:

Example activities and outputs

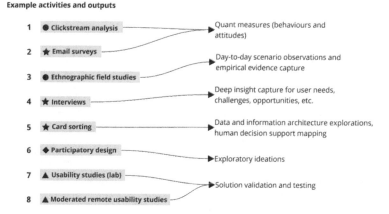

Let's break this down and add some context.

1. As a designer, you might start by **looking at existing quantitative data**. In this case, it could be the data that business stakeholders have already captured through the Google Analytics they had connected to the app. They also might have some **unstructured anecdotes, qualitative (but often incomplete) insights**, and assumption-driven hypotheses from before.

In this example, the team used a clickstream from the previously mentioned Google Analytics implementation. Depending on the current state of a product or service in hand you will want to dig deeper into the data at hand to get a sense of where the key challenges and opportunities lie.

2. From there, you might want to outline the variance in general usage of the app by uncovering more **insights about users' attitudes**. For the sake of an example, let's imagine that those hundreds of lab technicians are located in various countries around the world, and you decide to gather their input via an email survey. This is where you'd want to craft good enough questions to cover as much ground as possible so it can inform the next steps.

Needless to say, your steps 1-2 in research could be any other appropriate method based on what I've described to you so far. In other words, this approach is not a one size fits all, it's just where I would start in this particular case.

3-5. In my experience almost all businesses looking for UX help will think that the issue is with the tool usability and/or its look and feel. They will even go to depths to unpack the underlying quantitative data, make significant assumptions and ultimately end up at the point they started. That's because **they look at the data but don't understand the why's.**

Your goal here would be to propose something that would allow you to see a day in the life of any of the app's users. In this particular case example, **an ethnographic observation effort would give you a deeper insight into how lab technicians use the current app,** how they log their decisions, and the real challenges that prevent them from using it more often.

You would then want to interview the people you observed to **dig even deeper, as the underlying behaviours and attitudes can only be uncovered by asking the right questions.** Presumably, you'd lay out all the findings and map out the current experience to indicate which areas need improvement and which don't.

Let's imagine, in this fictitious case that:

- **The lab technician is too busy to always log in to that tool.**
- **The tool also logs them out automatically after 5 minutes.**
- **They also wear gloves that make it hard to use a touchscreen.**

Because of these simple limits, they are not keen to go out of their way to take off the gloves, wash their hands, login, go through several steps to type out their decisions and outcomes, put the gloves back on and continue with their work until the next time they make a decision that needs to be logged.

You can see that the key issues have very little to do with the UI or usability, even if every tool can be optimised to infinity. In other words, the look and feel of the application is not the challenge uncovered in research. The qualitative research should allow you to get more insights into the real-life challenges and peripheral touchpoints that keep users from contributing.

So while the business has most likely brought you in to redesign their web app, you need to feed those other experience points back to the immediate project team, product managers, business stakeholders, and others – this is what user experience design is about.

The real issues that the business now needs to address (at a bare minimum) based on the pain points we've uncovered are:

- **Performance:** Login that takes too long and logs the user out after five minutes
- **Tech:** Touchscreens that don't work when users wear gloves
- **Usability, information architecture, UI improvements** for the app to make it more intuitive and reduce the time it takes for the user to log their decisions

Note that in real projects, you'll find a lot more improvement areas along similar lines as the above examples. You'll need to advocate for, convince and help prioritise these insights with your team and the business stakeholders. This isn't always easy because those stakeholders have come in with preconceived notions about the challenges and their solutions.

Because you have done thorough research, however, you should be able to convince them using the data you have collected. Influencing others to follow your researched plan will be the hardest part for any UX doer who wants to design the right things and to design them right.

6. You can probably already think of ways to ideate and solve those three issues we've uncovered. That's exactly what you should do next, given you and your team know enough to proceed. Once you **ideate, prioritise, design and come up with a prototype, you'd want to test it**.

7-8. In this case, you could test your prototype remotely or in person. Let's say that you ran an ethnographic deep dive in person. Then you'd want to continue by running the tests in a similar way.

During the user testing part of user research, most entry-level designers tend to validate only the UI solution design. They rarely consider all the peripheral challenges and how the UI fits into the tasks users perform in their natural environment. That's why you'd want to come up with some hypotheses of what you're trying to find out, then test the end-to-end journey in the users' natural environment.

Furthermore, it would be best if you aimed to allow them to go through the same journey that they introduced you to initially, but this time using your redesigned solution as a prop.

Naturally, there are a ton of things that you must learn to run UX research properly, and this is just an example to clearly demonstrate some of the important items along the way.

$$\infty$$

FAQS

When do you know if you have researched enough?

As you develop your research skills, you'll start noticing patterns and areas of clarity, indicating that you know just enough to proceed with the next steps. If you can answer most of the following questions with YES, you probably have researched enough to start actioning it. In no particular order:

- Do the findings start to repeat and form different themes of insights?
- When thinking about the gaps identified before research, are they primarily filled in?
- Have you proven or disproven your hypotheses?
- Did you learn enough to start actioning the research?
- Did you cover most of your target audience (user archetypes) and applied the appropriate research methods?
- Are you running out of time for the allocated research efforts?

What about testing with five users as advised by the Nielsen Norman Group?

Based on Jacob Nielsen's guidelines[1] zero users will provide zero insights; meanwhile, around five people should uncover 75-80% of usability issues. After that you quickly hit the point of diminishing returns where testing with more people uncovers fewer and fewer problems yet still costs you time.

It's worth noting that Nielsen's principle also says that to reveal 100% of usability issues, you need to test with at least 15 users.

When running discovery efforts, you shouldn't plan them around a set number of users.

If you capture insights via quantitative measures, the more input you get, the better!

On a qualitative basis, what matters most is to focus on capturing the as-is experience in-depth and covering all the predefined user archetypes, so numbers are still important but not quite as much.

Ideally, you'd want to accumulate insights with each research effort. In discovery you might engage with 3, 5, 10, 20 or more people, but it all depends on the size of the problem at hand and on how diverse your user archetypes are.

For example, in the past I've run service design discoveries with 11 different personas and had to plan for engaging with over 50 different users mapping to these personas. Naturally, when it came to digital touch point validation and user testing a couple of different product designs, the audience was trimmed down to only a few people representing specific personas.

How to convince the business to do (or start doing) user research properly?

While not something you need to consider to get into UX, this is surprisingly a question I get asked both by new designers or researchers as well as by those with more experience.

I'm asked this so often that I made a video titled "What to do if your company doesn't allow for proper UX": https://bit.ly/CantDoUX. Make sure to watch it to understand better the point I'm about to make:

DO THE RESEARCH ANYWAY.

Presumably, if you struggle to involve users in your process, the business sees you as a UI producer rather than a specialist capturing valuable insights. There are a few paths to convince such companies of the value of research and they all take time. Try to slowly transition your personal ways of working, as well as those of your design or project teams toward user validation (testing) and then toward end-to-end user research activities.

If your stakeholders have preconceived notions about the problem or how to solve it, instead of fighting them, first collect evidence. It's easier to get buy-in for user research if you frame it as being necessary to validate those stakeholders' ideas, rather than questioning their beliefs right at the start of the project. Once you do the research and capture enough insights, then use the (sizeable) evidence to shift their attitudes and behaviours.

Because UX is a team sport, involvement from the stakeholders will be critical if you want to establish better, user-centred ways to solve their problems. It will take time, but it might be worth the challenge if you want to develop into a stronger UX practitioner and eventually a design leader.

---

1. *Why you only need to test with 5 users* by Jacob Nielsen, 2000: https://bit.ly/UserTest-With5Users

WHAT ABOUT DESIGN THINKING, DESIGN SPRINTS AND OTHER STREAMLINED DESIGN METHODS?

I'm a firm believer that every tool has its application. For example, industry-proven methods and frameworks do wonders for specific problems that certain organisations and cultures might have. However, they shouldn't be mixed up with user experience design, even if they contribute to the user or customer experience.

Particularly worthy of mention are the two most prominent frameworks that tech culture has adopted in recent years:

Google Design Sprints

Google's design sprint method can be good for a jam packed workshop that only allows a few days to outline and quickly test potential innovative solutions.

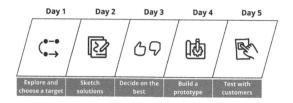

Day 1	Day 2	Day 3	Day 4	Day 5
Explore and choose a target	Sketch solutions	Decide on the best	Build a prototype	Test with customers

One aspect of design sprints that I do find beneficial is the ability to outline rough problem areas and frame them. It's something UX strategists could do, but junior and growing designers often miss this step.

Design Thinking

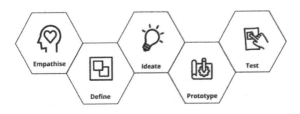

Great for: jam-packed workshops to get ideas flowing, driving a human-centred approach and employing empathy to advocate for the end-user needs. Design thinking workshops build momentum around rapid innovation and solution-oriented delivery.

Both frameworks are used for ideation efforts by consultancies, agencies and sometimes in-house product teams worldwide. These methods can break the ice well in an environment where innovation is stifled due to a lack of alignment over the product/service strategy, an absence of momentum and generally stale efforts to deliver impact.

But these strategies are not the silver bullet that can replace the proper UX process.

Jam-packing workshops and sessions to get to the solution as fast as possible also results in sacrifices. These usually come down to trimming the fat (visceral at that) for running deep user research.

Ultimately the issue with these methods is that they are based on the notion that everyone is a designer and that user research can be trimmed, or worse, sacrificed, for a quick, creative innovation effort. From the previous chapter, you should know that bypassing deep user research is extremely risky and costly and tends to result in stupidly limited solutions that lack traction and meaning.

When it comes to entry and junior level designers, it is common that I see them use these frameworks instead of real UX. This is often not the junior designer's fault, as they don't know any better if their teachers preach limited knowledge.

Human-centred design pioneer himself – Don Norman, who coined the term "user experience", notes that:

"... experts coming in and telling people what to do is also really paternalistic and doesn't work. Experts don't understand the local culture. They don't understand the abilities, skills, and real needs of the people they're trying to help. "[1]

Don also highlights how today's user-centric design usually includes the subject matter experts, but not the actual people that the problems are being solved for. This approach typically treats the symptoms rather than solving the root cause of the human problem.

While external consultants and designers can empathise by bringing people into workshops, **nothing beats the combination of strategic workshops and deep-rooted insights from appropriate user research efforts**.

Simply put, you should learn UX first and only then learn these streamlined frameworks as add-ons.

---

1. I recommend the following article to help you understand the not-so-subtle gap between a truly human-centric approach and today's streamlined design approach: https://bit.ly/donnormanempathy

PART 2

WHERE YOU'RE GOING

CHAPTER 2

PLAN YOUR FUTURE

"If you fail to plan, you are planning to fail!"

BENJAMIN FRANKLIN

Because of its scientific approach to understanding users, UX is much more about planning than it is about execution. In fact, executing design without planning and researching first is the exact opposite of what UX should be all about. This is true whether you want to specialise in product or service design, user research or any other subset of user experience.

Planning is not just a key step of the UX process. It's also a key step for you as someone who wants to get into the UX industry. Without a plan, you can't know what you're aiming for and you'll struggle to succeed.

To create a plan, I recommend first setting the BIG goals that would make your UX career a success. Then define the smaller incremental milestones along the way to the big goal(s). Finally, you should specify the very first steps towards that first smaller milestone.

To help you create this plan, I'll summarise some of the critical pieces of advice that I can share as an experienced UX professional and a hiring manager in the field. I'll give you a glimpse into what the UX world is like, what's required of you as a designer, and how long it really takes to become proficient.

Finally, I will also help you outline the future vision for how you can become a UX pro.

CONSIDER YOUR STARTING POINT

The key concerns I observe are the following (these are all actual questions I've received in the past):

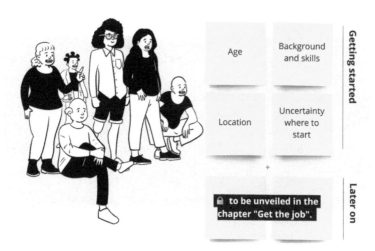

1. **Age-related**
2. *"I'm 45, is it reasonable for me to get started in UX?"*
3. *"I'm 21 and want to get into UX; what should I do?"*

1. **Background related**
2. *"I'm a nurse. How can I get into UX?"*

3. *"I'm a teacher and think a lot of skills are transferable; do I need UX experience to get into UX?"*

1. **Geographical location related**
2. *"I live in Ohio, what should I do to get a UX job?"*
3. *"Everyone is looking for UI/UX designers where I live, but I focus on UX rather than visuals; what should I do?"*

1. **Uncertainty about where to start**
2. *"Which UX course is the right one?"*
3. *"Is <insert UX bootcamp> worth it?"*
4. *"I'm considering applying for <insert a school name> programme. Is it any good?"*

I have just one answer to all of these: It doesn't matter who you are, or how old you are, or where you live, or what degree (or education) you have. Let's break down what hiring managers like me think about each of these concerns.

AGE-RELATED BLOCKERS

Make your age an advantage instead of a blocker.

If you're a mature candidate, you can highlight your experience in other jobs, especially when it comes to people skills, human interactions and collaboration. It's not a secret that the more commercial experience you have in any field, the more likely it is that your interpersonal skills are polished.

If you're a younger candidate, spend extra time and energy to pull together strong projects and case studies – let the work do the talking. Emphasise your freshness, enthusiasm, and willingness to learn and get the job done.

The point here is that you shouldn't be focusing on your age at all, focus on the experience and what you plan to bring to the table. Experienced hiring managers will not care about your age, but the evidence of the quality of your work. Trust me, this is coming from someone who has managed designers just out of high school, as well as designers who were twice my age.

BACKGROUND-RELATED BLOCKERS

Even when you're starting from scratch, you can relate your experience to UX no matter how disparate. Although most degrees and job experiences don't directly transfer into the real-world research and design scenarios, here's a few other disciplines which, if you have experience with them, could help you get into UX faster:

- Social sciences, human factors and psychology
- Any research-based studies (ethnography, anthropology, history etc.)
- Informatics, product and engineering and general tech studies
- Any creative fields that require you to build something from the ground up - however distant from UX (graphic design, signage, architecture, etc.)
- Business, marketing and communication
- And absolutely any major that involves working with others

If you aren't sure whether your existing skills are relevant in UX, see the diagram of UX disciplines in the earlier chapter titled "UX in a nutshell".

Having said all that, I've worked with juniors who transitioned into UX from careers in maths, law, catering services, taxi driving and more. I even worked with someone who'd been a lifeguard! Ultimately, it's not the degree that makes a great designer, but rather the skills they have acquired and how they use them.

A degree will not land you a job. University-level education in most cases today does not have a directly transferable path into a career.

I've seen juniors and apprentices who had no degrees but rather months of self-paced learning under their belts (bootcamps, online UX courses, books and YouTube videos, etc.). These people had more success landing their first job than others with master degrees but no fundamental knowledge of what UX is about.

Naturally, any expertise (formal or informal) will work as a foundation for learning other things. When it comes to user centric design though, you will still need to learn user centric design to be good at it.

LOCATION-BASED BLOCKERS

This blocker is the hardest to affect. Some locations (especially in the global north) do offer more UX opportunities than others. People already in those tech boom locations have more freedom to switch careers, to take risks in career progression and learning.

Not everyone will be that lucky. For the rest, there are a few clear pathways that you could take if you find yourself struggling to overcome location-based blockers:

Make the best of what you've got; Even if you don't live in Silicon Valley, New York, London or Dubai, there are still places and firms requiring skilled UX designers everywhere. They just don't know it yet. I've witnessed in the past that many companies outside the typical tech hubs look for UI and visual designers. They often label these roles with UI/UX. Often they don't know any better, but given the different contexts and varied needs of other markets, you mustn't blame them.

One aspiring UX designer reached out to me asking for advice precisely on this topic:

"I am a junior UI/UX designer based in Nigeria; it is so disappointing that the majority of startups and big tech companies don't even give attention to all these UX processes. Instead, they are all after the flashy and colourful UI designs."

My response?

"That's fine. Apply with UI, then do UX anyways.

It must become part of your process, and if you can, then use it to showcase the value. Then the business will buy into proper UX, but it will be a process that might take time."

If you choose this career path, then the most crucial question you must answer right now: what can you do with the tools you've got that will take you nearer to your goals?

- **Remote work:** Another option to explore could be remote positions that allow for distributed UX work. Granted, these opportunities are rare and will more often than not mean doing UI work instead of research-driven UX.
- **Migration:** I moved from Denmark to the UK for this exact reason – I realised I had very few options to do proper, deep UX work in my home country. Things are different now, but at the time there weren't many firms that could support my growth into a UX designer, rather than just having me do UI work day in and out.

The latter move was a hard decision to make, all things and risks considered, but it has paid off. I'm very aware that as a European, I'm too privileged to offer any advice on this matter, especially to someone who might be facing harsher conditions, or more difficulty leaving their country.

In the end, what's clear is that only you know what's suitable for you.

UNCERTAINTY ABOUT WHERE TO START

The last and the most straightforward blocker to address is uncertainty about where to start. Old-timers in the UX field figured things out on the fly. We learned from books, articles, mentors, apprenticeships and, more often than not, through trial and error. It took me a good decade to learn UX end-to-end, and there's still plenty I don't know.

Today, your learning journey could be shortened in half if you know what to look for. There are many learning sources of good quality, at a reasonable price and run by designers who understand what it takes to do UX properly.

In spite of the breadth of material (or maybe because of it), you might still feel lost. I wrote this book because I wanted to bring clarity to people like you. I wish I'd had a simple guide on how to get into UX design back in the day. In the following chapters, I'll share how you should approach picking your learning material, and I'll share some free and paid sources which would benefit any developing or experienced UX designer.

IN SUMMARY

What matters is what you plan to do to achieve your goal of getting into UX. It's easy to find reasons why you have a unique set of challenges but in reality, everyone has their own issues to deal with.

More often than not, these issues are internal blockers that you'll need to face head-on, leap over or smash through to move forward. If you're reading this book, I trust you have already made that decision to go all in.

∞

WHAT DOES IT TAKE TO BECOME A UX DESIGNER?

Let's start unpacking some of the core, technical, and soft skills that are an absolute must for any user experience designer and researcher.

I frequently use the following list with junior designers to help them understand where they are currently and what they should continue learning:

CORE OR TECHNICAL SKILLS

Research		Self evaluation
Planning and admin	User recruitment	*e.g. beginner I*
	Research session scheduling	
	Appropriate research method planning	
Discovery and generative research	Hypothesis generation	
	UX success criteria definition	
	As-is experience mapping	
	Competitive analysis	
Quantitative research	Analytics data analysis	
	Surveys (email, intercept)	
	Usability studies (unmoderated)	
	True intent studies	
	All other methods (advanced)	
Qualitative research	User interview observation	
	User interview facilitation	
	Ethnographic field studies	
	Usability studies (moderated)	
	Usability studies (remote, moderated)	
	Participatory design	
	Card sorting	
	Desirability studies (propositional)	
	All other methods (advanced)	
Actioning research	Research synthesis	
	Reporting and effective insights playback	

Definition & ideation		Self evaluation
	Divergent-convergent thinking	*e.g. advanced*
	How might we	
	Storyboarding	
	Ideation workshop planning	
	Ideation workshop facilitation	
	To-be experience mapping	
	To-be scenarios and flows	
	All other methods (advanced)	

Information architecture (IA)

	Self evaluation
Sitemaps	*e.g. expert*
Taxonomy: naming, data	
Systems thinking	
IA Principles	
IA user testing methods	
Visual and structural hierarchy	

Content design

	Self evaluation
Branding	*e.g.intermediate*
Colour theory	
Accessibility	
UX writing	

Interaction design

		Self evaluation
Human-computer interaction	Usability heuristics	*e.g. beginner II*
	Human-computer interface principles	
UI prototyping	Wireframing	
	UI design: fundamentals	
	UI design: pixel perfect / finesse	
	Responsive design	
	Mobile design	
	Interactive data visualisation	
	Prototyping macro interactions (flows, pages, components)	
	Prototyping micro interactions (elements)	
	Interactive motion design	
Design systems	Atomic design principles	
	Working with design systems	

"SOFT" AND META SKILLS

Soft and meta skills	Self evaluation
Empathy	*e.g. entry*
Anti-solutionising and challenging the status quo	
Giving constructive feedback	
Seeking design feedback	
Verbal and written communication	
Curiosity	
Storytelling	
Collaboration	
Teaching and evangelism	
Workshop facilitation	
Stakeholder management and influence	
Business acumen	
Leadership	
People management	

As you can see, there's a lot, and this isn't even a complete list of the skills you'll need to develop throughout your UX career.

Most of these can be developed over time but it's important to think about your larger end goal and then work backwards to identify the specific steps you need to take.

UNDERSTAND WHERE YOU STAND

As a first step, I recommend running through the list of skills in the previous section and self-evaluating based on your exposure to different UX skills.

Better yet, you can get a mentor or a more advanced designer who is familiar with your work to do this for you. This way, you will receive constructive feedback from an outside perspective on what your starting point is and what you have left to learn.

If you're doing it yourself, take a pen and going step by step, try to self-evaluate as best as you can. Use the following evaluation scale and make sure to check the criteria:

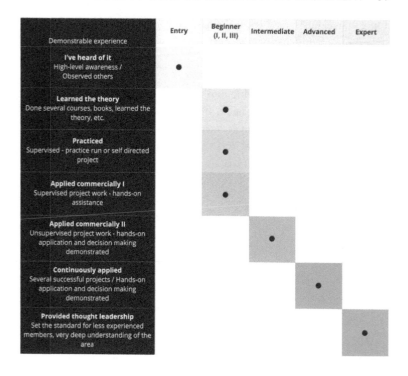

Demonstrable experience	Entry	Beginner (I, II, III)	Intermediate	Advanced	Expert
I've heard of it High-level awareness / Observed others	●				
Learned the theory Done several courses, books, learned the theory, etc.		●			
Practiced Supervised - practice run or self directed project		●			
Applied commercially I Supervised project work - hands-on assistance		●			
Applied commercially II Unsupervised project work - hands-on application and decision making demonstrated			●		
Continuously applied Several successful projects / Hands-on application and decision making demonstrated				●	
Provided thought leadership Set the standard for less experienced members, very deep understanding of the area					●

For best usability, I'd recommend viewing this resource on your desktop. You can download a PDF to print out from my website: https://bit.ly/GetIntoUXContent.

You've probably noticed that there are three beginner levels. This is done on purpose. That's because people who are just getting into UX will be somewhere between the entry and the third beginner level. I split these levels to make it easier to understand where you are now and to provide some incremental step-ups for your growth.

Pause here and complete the evaluation. Try to be as honest as you can. This activity isn't about your aspirations and where you want to get to, but rather it should be a brutally honest assessment of your skills as they are now.

Once you're done, step back and reflect on what else you need to improve. Take note of the current and next steps, and ideate how you will start practising the skills that are lacking.

Note that I will not be delving into the technical skills themselves as that is outside the scope of this book. It might take several books that you'll need to read in your own time to achieve this. Worry not, in the following chapters, I'll share some resources that you can choose from to cover any learning gaps you just identified.

∞

HOW MUCH TIME DOES IT TAKE TO GET INTO AND MASTER THE UX?

You've probably heard of the 10,000 hours rule.[1] It states that anyone who wants to master a skill needs to practice it for at least that amount of time.

For example, if you'd like to become a good enough UX designer, based on this rule you'd need to clock in a few years of full-time commitment to UX work.

But how accurate is this rule anyway?

It's not the number of hours that's important but understanding the fact that your journey will take time. Some designers might take 10,000 hours, others might take less or more. I've seen both outliers; those who got started with mere months of learning UX/UI and those who still can't call themselves a pro after years of honing the craft.

In the end, you might clock in 10,000 hours in just one area of UX before moving onto the next and so on. Again, the number of hours doesn't actually matter and is not always true. What you should take away from this is that you need to start as soon as possible because your journey will always take time.

I'd rather you start small, right now, and with a bigger goal in your mind than to focus on the many thousands of hours ahead of you.

If you aimlessly study UX concepts without a goal in mind, your many hours of work may multiply even more. Whereas if you spend the time intentionally, in a way that is aligned with your end goal, none of your hours spent will be wasted.

For example, my strategy for getting into UX was to gradually infiltrate the field. I knew I'd have to collect just enough of those hours so that, even if I didn't know UX well, I could start adding value while I learn. When my UX research skills were not yet up to par, I could still contribute and showcase my potential to employers in other ways.

To better illustrate this strategy, here are the tactics that helped me break into UX:

Education:
First I got two consecutive degrees: one in multimedia design and communication, the other in web development.

You do not need a degree to get into UX, but college education is definitely one route to help you learn what you need for the field. The real value of a college education is in meeting the professors and more skilled peers who you can learn from. Other than that, higher education can be replaced with a few good books and a handful of side projects.

Even before my degrees, I developed strong graphic design skills by crafting video game banners for old-school forums as a hobby. Developing peripheral skills like that in my free time boosted my skillset in UI and then in UX design.

Don't feel discouraged if you didn't start early like me. Simply take the advice that you should practise UI and UX wherever possible in your life to begin building up your experience, no matter your age or current career.

Making something every day:
While trying to finish those degrees... I spent most of my non-partying, non-part-time-job-lifting-heavy-crates hours further developing my skills in digital design, UI, iOS and web development, and user research.

One of the first things I did while gaining an education was to create a portfolio hosting all of my experimental work and learnings. This step, by far, was the most critical in setting my career up for success because it forced me to seek quality in outcomes rather than focussing on just the outputs. By the time I finished my degrees, I had collected a few strong cases I could use to get an internship or another junior designer opportunity.

Asking for the opportunities:
As I progressed with my learning, I kept doing freelance gigs here and there which I landed through cold emails. I offered cheap, sometimes unpaid services and used design marketplace sites to find more leads.

The gigs included creating then-popular Flash ads, coding websites and interactive games, producing videos, and more for national and international businesses.

However, I knew that I had to find a more formal environment to further my knowledge of UX. I emailed every single digital studio, agency and software house in Denmark that I could find on Google. Not at once; I compiled an Excel sheet and would email at least 10 of them every day. In my emails, I asked for an internship or apprenticeship opportunity, even when these companies didn't have any open design roles on their websites.

The emails were basic and to the point: "*Hey, I'm V. Here's my portfolio link. I would like to join your firm as a UI/UX intern because...*"

I did this for weeks until someone finally responded.

The first commercial placement:
I met with the founders of one company and showcased my WIP portfolio of mostly UI work with one UX case which I thought was strong at the time. And I got in.

From there on, I was doing my best to be a great intern, to learn and shadow others, while still working on my degree in web development. By joining a commercial environment early, I was able to tame my ego, gain some business understanding, and experiment with doing good UX work.

Becoming a junior UX designer:

Eventually, and probably because the job I was doing was not so bad, I convinced the firm to pay for my services. I became a client-facing UI/UX designer.

At that point, my UI skills were PRO (I was charging money to design interfaces), but as a UX designer, I would have been entry-level at best.

Inspired by the likes of Jacob Nielsen and Don "The Don" Norman, I decided to deepen my skills in user experience and human-computer interaction. This would help me transition into a more appropriate UX role.

So getting my foot in the door at a firm with UI work allowed me to support myself with paid work while also learning more about UX. I had a lot to learn and do before I could call myself a UX designer but I kept exploring other opportunities that would help me hone those skills.

---

1. The exact number of hours in this rule, originally featured in Malcom Gladwell's book *Outliers*, has been debunked in several studies afterwards. However, while the number of hours varies, it's still true that in order to master any specialty you will need to invest time.

REAL STORIES OF DESIGNERS AND HOW THEY GOT INTO UX

You've read how I got my first role as a junior UX designer, but I'm just one example. Paths into UX vary since everyone's journey has unique challenges and opportunities. To understand the sheer variance it's essential for you to see some other paths.

In the following few stories I'll outline at a high level the paths that junior designers who I've worked with took to get into the UX field.

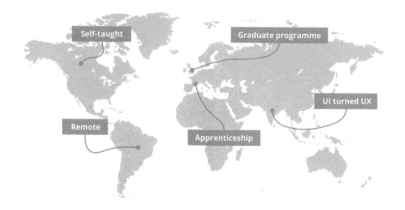

UK - GRADUATE PROGRAMME PLACEMENT IN A CORPORATE UX TEAM

During her graduate studies in social sciences, PY reached out to a programme advisor who had a network of big corporate organisations in the UK. She applied for an opening the advisor recommended, interviewed with them and, after passing several assessments, she got the job.

Graduate programmes help a graduate join an established company to learn as part of a structured and coached environment. Think of it as a paid internship or apprenticeship that's available to join once every year or so.

The best bit about this programme, and the reason PY got into UX, was that this programme had her rotate within the company from one business unit to the next at her own pace. PY started with working in project management and then project delivery, but neither of these specialities felt right for her. She thought a more creative team would be a better fit so she rotated to the UX team.

The UX team was used to working with entry- and junior-level employees, so they had established methods for exposing new joiners to the right learning materials, tools and practice. They welcomed her right off the bat. On this team she could immediately shadow and assist senior colleagues. Today, PY still loves working on this team and is trying to contribute even more, which to me sounds like a career UX designer in the making.

∞

CANADA - SELF-TAUGHT DESIGNER LANDS FIRST UX JOB

A business analyst by trade, AK has been 'artsy' all her life and loved to draw, craft and generally DIY things around her. Working on a project with a UX designer got her interested in creative problem solving and design outcomes-focussed research. AK had produced wireframes, written stories and technical specs before but not through this creative lens.

She researched many options to learn UX, but most of them were either too vague or too broad. Some were focused on UI, others on user research.

Then there were bootcamps, crash courses, online courses, etc. She took a few affordable ones on the weekends, but they didn't lead anywhere. AK realised that to get a proper UX role, she needed a portfolio and a case study which she struggled to come up with on her own.

A well-rated bootcamp came with a finished case study at the end and a guaranteed work placement afterwards. However, bootcamps can be expensive and after looking deeper, she read that the work placement was more of an internship with no promise of an extension. Instead, she doubled down on learning and producing a UX case study.

However, the project she worked on resulted in a very generic UX case study. With such a simple portfolio, applying for jobs didn't yield any job offers. AK noted that she might have aimed too high. She asked for my advice, and alongside her existing job, I recommended that she take up a side project or two that could showcase her ability to solve a variety of different (and more complex) problems. I told her to document the side projects in a case study and try applying again.

It took a few months (which she counted as commercial experience, and you can too if it's proper UX) but finally AK landed her first role as a junior UX designer using the new case study she had developed.

INDIA - COMPUTER SCIENCE STUDENT TURNED SELF-TAUGHT UI AND UX DESIGNER

RV was in his last year as a computer science major when he realised that product and UI design could be the right career for him. He was creating apps in his free time so he started watching YouTube tutorials to improve his UI design skills. He started applying UI kits, making his products responsive, and finally offered his services to other people.

After some time, RV got hooked on bringing ideas to life and played with the thought of doing this professionally. He started by looking into local ads. RV noticed that many of the job descriptions he saw with his skillset had something in common: UI/UX design.

To learn about UX, RV looked up videos on YouTube (that's how our paths crossed), online courses, and articles to deepen his understanding of the UX field. Unfortunately, this desire to learn landed him in tutorial hell: the never-ending cycle of learning without becoming skilled by actually applying those learnings in practice.

The wake-up call happened when RV missed the deadline for a job application because his portfolio wasn't ready. In all that time he'd spent learning, he'd never developed a portfolio which he now found to be critical to landing UI/UX roles.

It took him a little while to reflect and notice that most of the hard work was already done. While his portfolio was not the best in class compared to many other designers, it was good enough to start applying for other job openings. It took some time, but RV got an offer and is now working as a UI/UX designer.

While most of his work is just UI work, he is starting to apply more and more appropriate UX methods. Even if the employer and senior members don't value it, he's researching user needs to make better design decisions. He knows that he can use this role to pull together robust case studies involving UX to land a better opportunity.

∞

BRAZIL - A VISUAL/UI DESIGNER TURNED REMOTE UX DESIGNER

Unlike UI-focussed design, UX is harder to do remotely because it requires direct engagement with users. However, that doesn't mean it's impossible to work remotely as a UX designer. AP from Brazil had been freelancing for a few years as a UI designer, primarily focussed on visual design deliverables rather than research, so he was able to work from home.

One of his projects with a tech startup required more design input than he was used to. Product managers asked him to run a workshop with users. AP took them through critical issues, storyboarding the future, participatory design, some testing, UI iterations and so on. What made it rewarding and meaningful was the act of connecting with users and understanding them.

Over the months of applying more and more UX principles and techniques, AP was able to land more UX-focussed remote freelancing gigs with other startups, as he could now showcase his skills via a portfolio.

While there are methods he still needs to master, that one project pushed him out of his comfort zone and indicated that 'hey, this is something I can do, and it's rewarding'.

Working together in one of my mentorship catch-ups, and based on his current skills, AP assessed himself to be a late junior/early mid-weight UX designer. His portfolio now showcases the value he can deliver to any other startup – he stands out from the crowd of designers who are UI-focussed.

FRANCE - STARTING A NEW CAREER AS A UX APPRENTICE

ST knew of UX only in terms of interface design. She'd heard people use "UX" when describing bad products. Quite spontaneously, she researched it which sparked further interest in the field.

ST had built a solid accountant career over a decade of self-paced learning and hard work. She reached a point in her career where she was too tired to continue but felt too young to retire. ST was also aware that a simple retraining wouldn't keep her at the same seniority level or paycheck if she moved into a new field.

As with many people who have families, she felt that a sudden career restart wouldn't be possible. She'd need a more horizontal shift in an environment that would support her growth.

ST's approach to this career change was very structured:

1. She researched internship openings, apprenticeships and trainee placements.

2. She then cold-emailed UX professionals via LinkedIn and directly via their portfolios.

3. She got several responses, including from me, to first learn the theory, then apply it on real issues and document the journey into a solid case study or two.

ST didn't dwell on the advice too long. She spent a few months of her free time developing a rough case study showcasing her understanding of the UX process at a high level and how design activities tie into it.

She did another round of outreach and applications but this time she targeted all placements not just the ones that had an opening. Two responded, and one was a good fit where she could assist a senior designer at selected times, which kickstarted an apprenticeship.

IN SUMMARY: YOUR JOURNEY WILL BE DIFFERENT

"*It is better to follow your own path, however imperfectly, than to follow someone else's perfectly*" - The Bhagavad-Gita

The one thing I want you to take away from this chapter is to notice that it wasn't the learning sources that made these designers more hireable but the evidence that they can do the job.

Each had a completely different path into UX, often taking advantage of connections and peripheral opportunities to learn more and build a portfolio. They faced different variables, and so will you, however there are certain actions that they all took regardless:

1. **They put theory into practice**
2. **They solved real problems around them**
3. **They documented their solutions as UX case studies.**
4. **They focused on what truly matters.**
5. **They started way earlier than they thought they should.**

These steps prop up the journey into UX and as such they are important for you too. I'll unpack all of these steps throughout the book as they become more important to the stage of your journey.

Before you continue reading, reflect on what challenges are preventing you from getting a UX designer role today. What we'll do next is ideate and outline your ideal career path. To reduce overwhelm and ease progression, we'll work our way backwards from a big goal to define the smaller milestones.

∞

ENVISION AND DEFINE YOUR FUTURE SELF

"Sit down, grab a piece of paper, and write out a fantasy story of your life"

When I was just starting out, I knew that I'd want to do UX for decades to come. I still feel the same way, even if most of my work these days might be to deliver UX via the 10-20 designers I manage. That vision and certainty kept me committed to my path,

At the start of my path I knew it would take a few years of hard work before I could confidently call myself a UX designer. Of course, the times were different then, and many of the resources you can access as a new designer today didn't exist yet. So even though I was ambitious I had a realistic timeframe to achieve my goal of becoming a UX pro and I set smaller milestones to help me get there.

Even though you have more shortcuts and quality material at your fingertips today, you will still benefit from approaching your goals strategically, by setting BIG targets and outlining the criteria to achieve them, before you jump into the learning.

WHY DEFINING A CLEAR VISION IS SO IMPORTANT

While I believe that anyone can become a UX designer with enough hard work, I also think that the motivation and drive to do so has to come from the right place.

With your big goals and smaller steps defined clearly, all you need to do is commit to becoming a designer and then work hard to achieve it.

It could take months and years to grow into UX but as futurist Isaac Asimov noted, "*today's science fiction is tomorrow's science fact*". You need to project what you're after even if it feels like fiction right now. Having a constant reminder of your goal primes your mammalian brain to put in the effort to achieve it.

OUTLINE YOUR FUTURE VISION

Without sounding too new-age, what I'm talking about is the often-over-looked concept of vision boards: ideas in plain text, printouts, cut-out photos, sketches, anything that will act as a visual cue.

To do this right, set aside an afternoon to outline your vision for your ideal destination in the UX. Make sure to ideate where you picture yourself being in the next three, five, ten years. Put it all on a paper sheet in whatever shape or form be it drawing, gluing magazine cutouts or writing stuff in plain text. Don't limit yourself or your ideas. Express fully what you want to achieve in UX (and the rest of your life) even if it seems impossible.

Here are a few tips:

Unpack your underlying motivations

- To begin, answer this question: why do you want to be a UX designer or researcher? Then, ask another few whys until you can't go any deeper. If the final answer is money, then it's worth understanding that UX is lucrative only in the long term.
- Given the number of years and the hard work you'll need to

clock in, there are better options to achieve monetary success. If it's a genuine interest in making meaningful things or solving problems, then you should be able to get into UX.

Consider progress in technology

- For example, many different and unrelated fields and different emerging tech industries might converge. Having started in web design for brochureware and e-commerce sites, I'm now working on a variety of complex services and apps using big data, machine learning and AI.
- The purpose and application areas changed, but the underlying UX with a human-centric and user-focused approach hasn't changed. Perhaps your future vision will look similar: UX design for digital UI-less neural UI solutions? Designing for AI-driven services? Designing for self-evolving machinery? A blockchain-based UX revolution? Humane and ethical design for the greater good? Sustainable tech?

You might already be picturing something exciting. But don't stop here; check out the full infographic showing different areas where you could practice UX.

Which of these would you love to be involved in?

Rotate book for the best reading experience

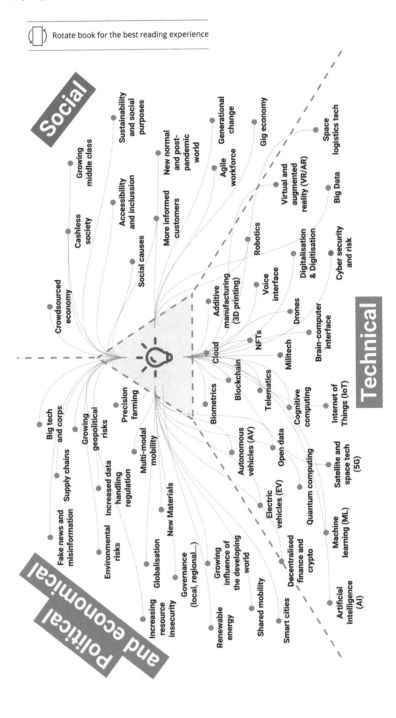

Social:

- Crowdsourced economy
- Gig economy
- Growing lower and middle classes
- Cashless society
- Accessibility and inclusion
- Sustainability
- Social causes
- More informed customers
- The new normal and the post-pandemic world
- Agile workforce
- Generational change

Technical:

- Artificial intelligence (AI)
- Decentralised finance and crypto
- Electric vehicles (EV)
- Quantum computing
- Machine learning (ML)
- Satellite and space tech (5G and beyond)
- Open data
- Biometrics
- Blockchain and distributed ledger
- Cloud
- NFTs
- Militech
- Cognitive computing
- Internet of things (IoT)
- Brain-computer interface (neural UI)
- Drones
- Voice UI
- Additive manufacturing (3D printing)
- Robotics and automation
- Digitalisation & digitisation
- Cyber security and risk
- Big data
- Mixed, virtual and augmented reality (MR, VR, AR...)

- Space logistics tech

Political and economical:

- Big tech and corporations
- Supply chains
- Growing geopolitical risks
- Fake news and misinformation
- Environmental risks
- Increased data handling regulation
- Precision farming
- Multi-modal mobility
- Globalisation
- Increasing resource insecurity
- Governance (local, regional, national, global... space)
- Renewable energy
- New materials
- Growing influence of the developing world
- Shared mobility
- Smart cities

And many more...

That's a lot to scan through so take a moment to reflect on which of these areas resonate with you more than others.

Consider your professional career path:

- Do you see yourself as a researcher or craftsman designer? Would you take the seniority or the leadership path? Or would you like to be someone who champions UX by delivering excellent solutions for years to come?
- It's ok for your ideas to evolve over time. When I started, I thought of being a UX designer, period. As I developed new skills, I realised that I wanted to deliver through others – this is how I discovered that in the long term, I'd like to become a design leader.

Consider your unique circumstances:

- This is the trickiest part. You might want to outline the geographical place, perhaps a specific city or tech hub, the culture you want to be part of, the types of solutions you want to deliver. Anything that resonates with you in the market, given the circumstances you face today, should be noted.
- Take a sheet of paper and write a paragraph describing the following two things: Firstly, where you'll work (industry, geographical place, organisation type, design team, etc.). Secondly, what sort of work you'll be doing and how your life will look from the peripheral standpoint.
- If any of the above are hard to define, **pick a role model or a UX person whose footsteps you'd like to follow**. When I started my journey, my role model was (and still is) designer Jesse James Garett. He wrote the must-read book "*The Elements of User Experience*" which helped me decide how I wanted my future to look.

I expect that some people will roll their eyes at this exercise as being some spiritual woo-woo. Instead see this exercise as a personal commitment – a manifesto that you plan to carry on to achieve your goals, get into UX and develop even further.

Visualisation and future-oriented imagination have been studied for their impact on sports[1] performance and creativity[2]. It is safe to say that people who proactively visualise their future are more likely to act, and achieve it. By visualising what they want to happen, they effectively create new neural pathways in their brain and prime themselves to complete what they've visualised.

Once you're done with your vision board, pause and think about what steps you need to take to achieve every one of the items on there.

Let all this information fuel you for the things to come. Because what comes next is learning, practicing and solving problems to break into the field of UX.

∞

1. *The effects of a Cognitive Intervention Package on the Free-Throw Performance of Varsity Basketball Players during Practice and Competition*: https://journals.sagepub.com/doi/abs/10.2466/pms.1992.75.3f.1243
2. *The Richness of Inner Experience: Relating Styles of Daydreaming to Creative Processes*: https://www.ncbi.nlm.nih.gov/pmc/articles/PMC4735674/

PART 3

HOW TO GET THERE

CHAPTER 3

GAIN A DEEP UNDERSTANDING OF UX

"It is important to view knowledge as sort of a semantic tree — make sure you understand the fundamental principles, i.e. the trunk and big branches, before you get into the leaves or there is nothing for them to hang on to."

ELON MUSK

There are several factors that impact how we capture information and make it accessible when we need to act on it. For example, picking the right learning material matters more than consistent and accumulative learning. However, there are methods that can boost your learning and ensure knowledge retention regardless of the material.

One of these methods is instructor-led social learning. Learning with others can help new designers like you connect the dots while practicing the craft, and help you recall information better in the future.

In this chapter you'll find several other methods that are proven to make absolutely any learning material worth the effort. Additionally, I'll introduce a handful of tools that can make the actual act of learning super-charged. For example, you'll find a simple framework that can make you 2x better at any skill every 72 days.

As with the previous chapters, take your time. Pause and reflect where necessary to fully understand the importance of the information read. This chapter will be critical to further developing your UX skills.

RETHINK YOUR LEARNING

"The internet lets you skip the career and go straight to your dream job"

SAHIL LAVINGIA

Let me start by using a simple analogy that has helped several junior designers restructure their approach to learning.

Consider this: The knowledge and skills you acquire fuel a virtual rocket that will get you to UX. All rockets come with several fuel tanks; there's always a set of booster starter tanks that carry the ship up to a certain threshold in its journey. Then the second type of fuel tank takes over; this tank is bigger and is meant to sustain the rocket's movement forward.

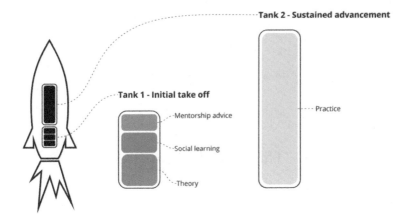

Neither of these fuel tanks is more important than the other but they need to be used in a purposeful sequence. For example, you can't just burn through the second giant tank of fuel because your ship would aimlessly burn out. You also can't just use the small booster tank and ignore the rest because your rocket will never breach the atmosphere.

The tanks are similar to your learning. The booster tank or tank 1 contains at least three compartments:

- **Acquiring theory**
- **Learning with others**
- **Getting support and guidance from mentors and more experienced designers**

Meanwhile, the bigger tank or tank 2 represents an immense amount of consistent practice: the years of trial and error that you must prepare for.

So when you think about how to approach your learning and getting into UX, use this model. Start with your first tank and fill it up incrementally so that each of the compartments is full enough. Then fill up the second tank with practice.

The analogy doesn't end here, though. **You should refuel those tanks constantly and reassess at which stage of the journey and skill maturity you are.**

∞

HOW TO PICK THE RIGHT
LEARNING MATERIAL

Out of the hundreds of messages I receive weekly, half are about which course, bootcamp or degree can help someone become a UX designer.

There isn't a single degree that will turn you into a designer overnight. You'll have to accumulate knowledge in a structured and planned way.

After all, as a UX designer, you will start every project by accumulating knowledge through discovery and planned user research efforts. You can apply these same methods to your learning progression now.

A typical learning progression that relies on readily available and paid learning material will look like this:

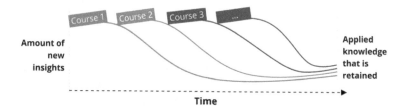

When experienced designers say that UX is a life of learning, this is what they are describing. The fat tail to each of the courses represents the rough rate of retention and recall. So regardless of what course you commit to now, you will need to "refill" your knowledge again over time with other courses, social learning methods and bite sized information.

When it comes to suggesting a specific course, the first piece of advice I give is to consider the four specific variables that are unique to every individual: **time, price, quality and your commitment to learning.** The perfect learning option for you should lie somewhere between these variables:

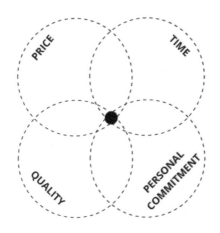

PRICE AND PERSONAL COMMITMENT TO LEARNING

There are clear pros and cons to both the free and paid learning options. In the end it is entirely up to you and your circumstances to decide which of the routes (or a combination) is right for you.

Findings from marketing and psychology[1] indicate that investing money into something keeps people more motivated and committed to it. This is also known as the 'marketing placebo effect'.

Studies have even shown that people don't just undervalue the things that cost less money, but they experience less efficacy from them. For example, people who bought energy drinks at a discount in one study reported feeling less energised than after consuming the same product at a higher price.

Even if you know about this bias and you know that the higher cost isn't necessary, sometimes you might benefit from investing money into your learning.

On the other hand, there are so many great resources that are freely available as courses, books, and other material. Much of this is created by experienced designers who want to help those new to the field.

These free learning resources are great when you need a quick answer or when you have a specific problem at hand. For example, suppose you want to know more about how to do journey mapping. In that case, you can go on YouTube and look at a practical example video or you could search for an article.

The key issue with free resources is that you'll be responsible for keeping up your commitment and momentum with it. There's no placebo and sometimes there's no further help either; you will need to keep yourself accountable as well as troubleshoot and find solutions the hard way.

Consider your personal circumstances and your budget. Ideally you'd want to invest into your learning if you can in order to stick with it, and you'd also want to use the many free resources to supplement the core learnings. Plan and allocate your budget accordingly.

QUALITY AND TIME

The quality of the course and the time you'll give it are two other considerations you must take into account. Below is a simple checklist to help you consider and make a more informed decision. If the course you're looking at ticks all these boxes, it might be a good option to take (provided that you can afford it).

Firstly, is this learning opportunity teaching true UX with a user research focus, or is it just a UI-focussed course with a fancy UX label?

It's essential to know this before you invest in a paid course or a boot camp. Check the curriculum to understand the depth of content. Better yet, run the curriculum by a more senior UX designer or mentor.

Courses that highlight user research tend to deliver quality throughout the material and are more likely to contribute to your growth into UX. I'd recommend even reaching out to the course makers to find out what user research methods they will teach you.

Some might do simple surveys and call them user research. While surveys are a valid research method, they should be supplemented by more mixed methods already outlined in the chapter "There is no UX without UX research".

Does it have weeks or months worth of well-paced material?

As per example above with course fat tail ends, for the knowledge to really sink in, it's best to learn over an extended amount of time. Also, it takes months and years to achieve proficiency in user experience skills. Make sure to find an option that will force you to invest not just money but also time.

Does it have a community, i.e. can you learn with and from others?

You need a community, however remote, to boost your progression through organic discussions and peer-to-peer feedback loops. A college degree is not required but it provides you with a ready-made community. Try to find a course or program like that which involves interaction with others.

Does it provide networking options (during and after the course)?

Networking options might include LinkedIn networks, the ability to connect with the alumni of the program or with mentors who can challenge and support you, etc.

Is it project-based so you can apply the theory and develop new skills in practice?

Unless you are a complete beginner who doesn't have a grasp on basic UX concepts, you should steer away from paid courses that only cover concepts, methods and best practices. Without practicing in a project-based setting and applying your skills, the course will be useless in making you a UX designer. Look for options that will force you to put EVERY-THING into practice.

Will it help you come up with UX case studies as part of the curriculum?

Following up from the previous point, it's important that the paid opportunity helps you collect evidence for your portfolio. If I could go back in time, the only reason why I'd opt for a bootcamp is that most of them promise you'll graduate with a case study in hand.

Will it need you to engage with actual stakeholders, and in particular real USERS?

This is a big one. I've interviewed some juniors in the past who have done bootcamps where their business stakeholders and users were... other students. So, what they learned in their course was to fake the project, fake the research, mock test the outcomes. You don't have to take a class to fake it. Find a course that has actual external partners to work with so you get real life experience.

Will it keep you accountable, engaged and in check?

When choosing your course, research how the teachers will ensure that you stick with it. Later on in the chapter "Learn UX skills faster", I'll go into more depth on why accountability is essential for anyone working towards their big goals.

Does it have a strict final assessment and evaluation with further feedback for improvements?

A lot of paid options also grant you a digital diploma with a fancy design. They use graduation imagery to give off credibility. However, a diploma with a fancy signature is useless as evidence that you are a UX pro — it only proves your attendance.

Ensure that the course you choose has a proper assessment with criteria you must meet to finish it successfully. On your resume, a note that you passed the course with a high percentage grade will have more weight than just an attendance diploma.

---

1. Placebo Effects of Marketing Actions: Consumer May Get What they Pay For; *Journal of Marketing Research*, 2005: https://stanford.io/3Eg8ryA

THE READILY AVAILABLE AND FREE LEARNING MATERIALS

Let's start with a quick rundown of the totally free and readily available resources. These can be split into the following four categories:

- **Free online and in-person courses**
- **Microcontent: articles**
- **Microcontent: YouTube**
- **Microcontent: podcasts**

FREE ONLINE AND IN-PERSON COURSES

Courses require a significant commitment to show up and progress with the learning material in a predefined sequence. You should create a learning plan that includes at least a few of the following options:

- Springboard: Free UX design curriculum
  - https://bit.ly/spBoardUX
- Gymnasium: UX Fundamentals - http://bit.ly/gymUX
- A variety of courses on Coursera, e.g.: Georgia tech: Intro to UX - https://bit.ly/georgiaUX
- Invision: Principles of UX design - http://bit.ly/invisUX
- Future Learn: Digital Skills and UX
  - http://bit.ly/futureLearnUX
- A variety of courses on Linkedin/Lynda (free trial

month): http://bit.ly/linkedinUX
- A variety of free lessons (tasters) on Udemy
  - http://bit.ly/udemyFreeUX
- Udacity: Intro to the design of everyday things by Don
  Norman - http://bit.ly/udacitydonnorman
- Udacity: Product design by Google
  - http://bit.ly/udacityGoogle
- A variety of lessons on Hack design - https://bit.ly/hackUXD

Plus a few more resources from yours truly:

- Product design with Sketch - http://bit.ly/sketchProductD
- Axure RP rapid prototyping masterclass
  - http://bit.ly/axurePrototyping
- Playlist about UX career development covering a variety of
  topics - http://bit.ly/careerInUX

You can also search 'free UX courses' online, and you'll find plenty of other resources you could start with.

∞

MICROCONTENT: ARTICLES

Microcontent is snippet-sized learning material that is great for learning specific skills or finding solutions to problems in UX. It's a running joke in the development community that to be a good coder, you need to know how to google well. The same applies to learning UX design.

User experience disciplines are too vast to learn everything upfront, especially when some activities you might do only in specific cases. Every pro I know regularly scans the headlines to get a quick insight into new research, case studies, tools, and so on. This is probably the easiest way to stay up to date with the field.

You might already have a few favourite blogs of your own. I'd advise you to add the blogs below to your list and start visiting them regularly. Feel free to also look for other specialised resources that focus on UX, product design and everything in between.

- UX Collective on Medium - http://bit.ly/UXCollective
- UX Mastery - http://bit.ly/UXMasteryBlog
- Smashing magazine - http://bit.ly/SmashingMagBlog
- Designmodo - http://bit.ly/DesignModBlog
- UX Booth - http://bit.ly/UXBoothBlog
- UX Movement - http://bit.ly/UXMovementBlog
- Invision blog - http://bit.ly/invInsideDesign
- Nielsen Norman Group articles - http://bit.ly/NNGBlog
- Desk magazine - https://bit.ly/deskMagazine
- UX Matters - https://UXMatters.com
- UX Planet - https://UXPlanet.org
- Yours truly - https://vaexperience.com

MICROCONTENT: YOUTUBE

As of 2021, YouTube is still the 2nd largest search engine on the Internet. The number of people who stream their videos in a specific niche grows by the day: UX is no exception. You probably found me and this book via the VAEXPERIENCE Youtube channel.

There's many YouTube channels that cover general UX, tutorials for processes and tools. Notable examples include:

- UX Mastery (UX) - http://bit.ly/YTUXMastery
- Nielsen Norman Group (UX) - http://bit.ly/YTNNGGroup
- Think like a UX researcher (UX research)
  - http://bit.ly/thinkLikeUX
- Delta CX (UX) - http://bit.ly/deltaCX
- Robert Smith (UX) - http://bit.ly/robertSmithUX
- Sarah Doody (UX) - http://bit.ly/sarahDUX
- Neuron (UX) - http://bit.ly/YTNeuron
- Mike Locke (UX) - http://bit.ly/mikeLockeUX
- CareerFoundry (UX) - http://bit.ly/YTCareerFoundry
- Kevin Liang (UX research) - http://bit.ly/kevinUXResearch
- Yours truly (UX) - http://bit.ly/vaexperience

There's a lot of channels that, even if they say they are about UX, actually only show the surface layer (UI focus) and don't cover the proper UX design and research process. Don't fall for this "bubblegum" content.

Remember that UX is a messy and brutally hard job; your learning material should reflect the real challenges of the role and demonstrate appropriate research-driven methods.

If I were you, I'd subscribe to all those channels I shared. There is value in passive learning through entertainment and hearing others' personal experiences. It can challenge your own presumptions and it'll help reinforce the things you know well enough already. YouTube also has many features to help you consume this content and learn: you can create playlists, sort videos by purpose, relevance, and so on. I'd recommend keeping a list of all the videos you find helpful.

MICROCONTENT: PODCASTS

Depending on your circumstances, you might also benefit from listening to learning content in the form of podcasts. Below are some of the options I am recommended by fellow design leaders:

- What is wrong with UX: http://bit.ly/wrongUX
- UX podcast: http://bit.ly/podcastUX
- UX & growth podcast: http://bit.ly/UXGrowth
- Boagworld UX Show: http://bit.ly/boagUXShow
- The UIE podcast: http://bit.ly/UIEPodcast
- NNG UX podcast: http://bit.ly/NNGPodcast
- Design better: http://bit.ly/invisionPodcast
- UK government digital service: http://bit.ly/GDSPodcast
- Mixed methods: http://bit.ly/mxMethods
- User defenders: http://bit.ly/userDefenders

… And many more.

THE PAID LEARNING MATERIALS

Let's start with a quick rundown of learning materials you have to pay for. These can be split into two categories:

- **The proven content: books**
- **Paid degrees, bootcamps and courses**

Please note that I'm not affiliated with any of the authors, organisations or resources that I list on the next few pages, save for the ones that I've created myself. These are industry-acclaimed sources that I've either tried myself, taken note of on resumes from high-performers, or heard positive feedback about from other growing and established designers.

THE PROVEN CONTENT: BOOKS

Writing a book is an arduous effort that takes time so you can expect the majority of books on UX to be high quality. They are usually written by people who have poured into them years or decades of their own experience.

So out of all the paid options, books are probably the cheapest way yet still effective way to learn theory. Effectively, you get a manual for a specific UX area written by someone who has been through trial and error so that you won't have to.

There's so many books about UX and design. My own library contains hundreds of them, covering UX, technology, innovation and business, all of which tie into experience design. It can be hard to know where to start, even if you only look at the top-rated titles.

I have two recommendations for you on where to start.

One, I list the UX-related books I read on my blog, along with a 1-5 rating for each: https://bit.ly/DesignReadingList

Two, I'm including this handpicked list of **the top titles that any entry or junior level designer should read:**

1. *100 Things Every Designer Needs to Know About People* by Susan M. Weinschenk
2. *The User Experience Team of One* by Leah Buley
3. *Lean UX* by Jeff Gothelf
4. *Think like a UX researcher* by David Travis
5. *The Elements of User Experience* by Jesse James Garrett
6. *Understanding Context: Environment, Language, and Information Architecture* by Andrew Hinton
7. *Just Enough Research* by Erika Hall
8. *Universal Principles of Design* by William Lidwell, Jill Butler, Kritina Holden
9. *Universal Methods of Design* by Bella Martin, Bruce M. Hanington
10. *Articulating Design Decisions* by Tom Greever

At the beginning of your UX career journey, you should be reading UX books like there's no tomorrow. So, here's a challenge to everyone who is just getting started: **pick up one book a week and read it from cover to cover.**

Most importantly, as you read, spend time applying and sharing what you've learned. Make sure you're taking notes, sharing your learning with others, and thinking through each concept and how it can be applied.

If you follow this challenge, you'll be able to read and learn from over 50 books in a year! That's sure to set you on a good path. Just don't get so caught up in reading that you never apply what you read in practice or create case studies!

∞

PAID DEGREES, BOOTCAMPS AND COURSES

Let's start with this common question I get from entry-level designers about bootcamps is: *will this bootcamp land me a UX job?* The answer: unlikely.

Even if some of the bootcamps out there now offer temporary job placements, they are far from being a secure option that many juniors are after. Bootcamps and intensive courses are there for you to LEARN ABOUT UX. **But no hiring manager will give you a job just for knowing about UX.** That is why you need experience and evidence that you can do the job in commercial scenarios.

As with any other learning material out there, what will matter is how you act on the learned information and what ends up in your portfolio. Granted, a lot of courses and bootcamps give you an option to start working on a portfolio UX case study immediately. Still, they rarely are at the quality required for junior positions (remember the 1–3-year commercial experience requirement?).

Don't get discouraged though. Courses can be worth it if you can afford them but make sure to translate theory into practical skills (and the documented assets into evidence for your future portfolio).

Paid self-paced online courses:

- Coursera - https://coursera.org
- Future Learn - https://futurelearn.com
- Interaction design foundation - https://interaction-design.org
- EdX - https://edx.org
- Udemy - https://udemy.com
- Skillshare - https://skillshare.com

- Pluralsight - https://pluralsight.com
- LinkedIn Learning (formerly known as Lynda.com) - https://linkedin.com/learning
- Treehouse - https://teamtreehouse.com
- UX Design Edge - https://uxdesignedge.com
- UX training.com - https://uxtraining.com

Paid online and in-person bootcamps:

- Ironhack school - https://ironhack.com
- Flatiron school - https://flatironschool.com
- General assembly - https://generalassembly.com
- Designlab - https://trydesignlab.com
- Career Foundry - https://careerfoundry.com
- Red Academy - https://redacademy.com
- Springboard - https://springboard.com
- Niche and specialised options, such as the Clinical UX Academy bootcamp that is focused on healthcare UX: https://www.clinicalux.org/

… And many more, just an online search away.

These lists are by no means an endorsement – you still must do your research before committing. Perhaps you'll find an even better option out there.

∞

THE NETWORK EFFECT: WHY LEARNING FROM (AND WITH) OTHERS IS SO POWERFUL

Did you know that instructor-led and collaborative learning is generally more effective than learning on your own?[1]

From my experience, learning with others will significantly boost your confidence and decision-making immediately. For one, when you're alone you're unlikely to make bold decisions, take calculated risks or experiment with a method you just read about. Learning with others can help push you and, additionally, sometimes you can avoid the costly trial and error by observing others go through it.

I used to share my learnings with fellow study mates and friends over coffee. They weren't as enthused but doing this helped me process what I read and make sure that I could explain it to others—a sort of a litmus test.

It may sound silly, but vocalising what you've learned truly is a key part to understanding and remembering[2]. Even just talking out loud to yourself in the mirror will help so if you don't have access to other people who would support you, try that solo technique.

After you do this, however, you still need to follow up with practical work to really digest the learnings.

HOW TO LEARN FROM AND WITH OTHERS IN DESIGN

There are a couple of things you can try to create a better learning experience for yourself:

1. **Find a mentor (virtually or in person), or access mentorship by proxy.** It will help you to have access to someone who's been there and done that, ideally with only a small degree of separation in experience from you. If they're too senior to you, their advice might not be as actionable in your current circumstances.

With a mentor you will still need to do the hard work, but they can nudge or provide clarity to help you get unstuck.

2. **Find design communities online or in-person.** Being part of a community and engaging in conversations, participating in meet-ups, conferences, etc., has been a critical part of my growth as a UX designer.

While you shouldn't compare yourself to other designers, being part of a community of designers can also help you gauge if your skills are right for what the industry needs. It can also help you stay motivated on this nonlinear journey you are undertaking.

There are other variations to these two suggestions for learning with others, but the core effect is that you need to be able to observe someone and learn socially. Combine the two methods, and you'll further accelerate your learning.

Understandably, finding a mentor or a community can be daunting so let's explore how you can do that. I'll also give you specific recommendations to get the most out of networking with others.

---

1. Learning collaboratively has been shown to increase student exam scores. Effectiveness of instructor-led collaborative learning in the classroom, 2015: https://bit.ly/learningwithothers
2. Vocalising the information has been shown to outperform other methods, such as just reading or reading and writing things down. Exploring long-term modality effects: Vocalization[sic] leads to best retention: https://bit.ly/vocalisetoretain

FIND A MENTOR

"Mentorship is similar to friendship. A mentor is someone who always makes time for you. It's not a one way street, it's an opportunity to learn from each other and grow together."

SIMON SINEK

Throughout my career, several people helped me get unstuck at different points. My friends, work peers, bosses, members of the UX community and even people I coached. At the time, I wouldn't have called any of these people my mentors. But looking back now, I can see that they were. My best mentors were people with whom mentorship happened organically, as a result of building a great working relationship first.

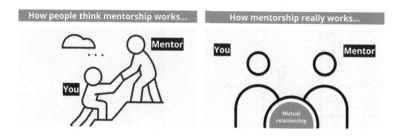

Rotate book for the best reading experience

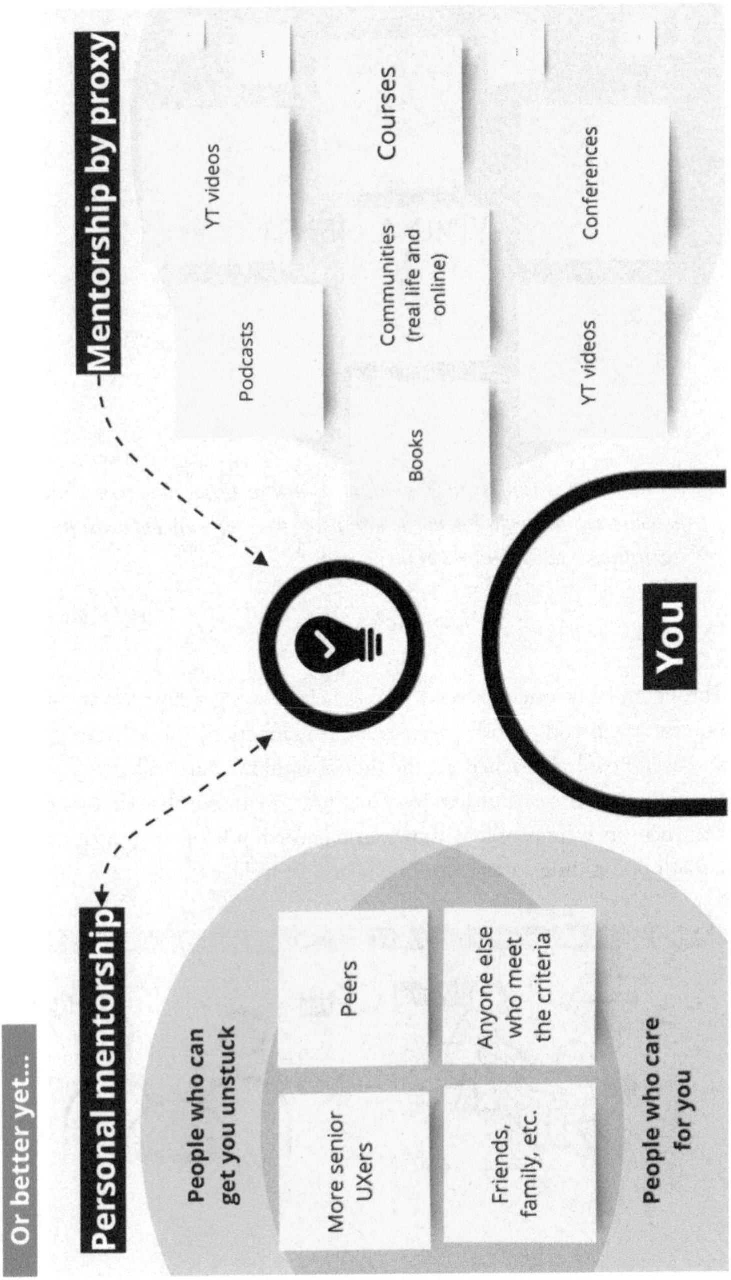

Mentorship by proxy

YT videos

Podcasts

Courses

Communities
(real life and
online)

Books

Conferences

YT videos

You

Or better yet....

Personal mentorship

**People who can
get you unstuck**

Peers

More senior
UXers

Friends,
family, etc.

Anyone else
who meet
the criteria

**People who care
for you**

In the image above you'll notice two distinct types of mentorship:

- **Personal mentorship**: what most people think of when talking about a mentor-mentee relationship.
- **Mentorship by proxy**: a label I like to use for the more modern approach of acquiring the information you need to get unstuck.

These two types are not incompatible. It's almost guaranteed that in your career you'll start with mentorship by proxy, as you take in different information and learning material, before you seek out more focussed advice from a mentor.

In the following pages I'll explain how to approach finding mentorship so that you build lasting relationship and are able to get advice anytime.

PERSONAL MENTORSHIP

The mistake I see most juniors make is reaching out to people cold asking them to be their mentor. The response to cold requests will always be a no; they are too transactional and lack authenticity.

Mentoring someone is a big commitment and even I can't mentor more than a couple of people at a time. (That's actually why I started my Youtube channel - to help as many people at once as possible.)

It might seem counterintuitive but **if you want to find a mentor, don't ask people to be your mentors.** When you do this, you're asking a stranger to do the work for you, free of charge. That stranger is busier than you are, so any request from you will compete with whatever else they have going on in their lives. You'll just come across as someone who wants other people to drop everything to focus on their needs.

But that's not how human relationships work. Your goal should be to build trust and a long-term relationship.

Chances are you probably already trust the potential mentor from their presence online or in-person, but do they trust you? Probably not, as presumably they don't even know who you are.

You need to start small and build a relationship over time. I recommend to take the same approach you would with new friendships: start slow, keep in touch, be patient, and allow for the relationship to develop organically.

If the person is a public thought leader in UX it could be that you'll be their biggest fan leaving comments on the content they produce in the beginning. As time goes on, if the things you contribute resonate with them, they will reciprocate.

The same applies to people you already know. Chances are you might have done a course, taken a bootcamp or participated in some webinar or meet-up where you've connected with a more senior UX designer or researcher. The approach to get mentored by them would be similar. It will come down to initially giving a lot more value than receiving which is how you earn trust. It takes time.

∞

HOW TO REACH OUT TO PROSPECTIVE MENTORS

Now that you know the key to forming a meaningful and mutually rewarding mentor-mentee relationship let me share some specific tips for reaching out to people.

Assuming no prior relationship, I'd expect you to cover the following points in your email (and to do so briefly):

1. **Introduce yourself** - where are you in your life and what are you after in the long term?
2. **Show enough humility** - why are they a good role model for you?
3. **Provide them with value** instead of asking for something immediately - what can you do for them? You might think that you have nothing to offer because you're just starting out, but that's not the case. You can still contribute, provide feedback, ask specific questions and otherwise engage with the prospective mentor. It doesn't take much to spark new relationships.

4. **Be succinct** in what you want - what input do you need from them?

5. **Adapt to their lifestyle** and time dependencies - how much time do you think you'll need? And how can you make sure to adapt to their busier schedules?

6. **Anticipate problems** and have a plan B if your mentor can't support you for whatever reason – where can you find solutions besides your mentor? They won't always be available.

7. **Always follow up** regardless of the outcome, but also make sure to action whatever they suggest and reflect - why was their advice valuable and what have you learned?

Here's an example of someone reaching out to me for mentorship and my responses. This type of simple back and forth developed into a working relationship. The numbers in the first example represent the above points you should aim to cover:

The 1st cold reach out:

"Hi V,

I've been following your work for some time now and just wanted to reach out to thank you. Your videos are great! [1][3]

I just started working as a junior designer [1], and the video on doing UX, even if the business doesn't want it, was very inspiring. I do struggle with that a lot as I'm the only designer in the team. [2]

I'd appreciate it if you could give me some advice to help with my UX skills development. I want to learn more about picking the right UX research methods. [4] Would you be able to have a virtual coffee in the next two weeks? I promise I wouldn't take more than 15mins of your time [5].

I know you must be very busy [5], but any pointers, doesn't matter how small, would help me a lot [6].

Thanks,
BT"

My response:

"Hi BT,

    Thanks for the kind words. Glad you find the content helpful.

I don't have much spare time at this point, but as a first thing to check would recommend you to look up the NNG article on picking the research methods - it's very clearly outlined. Also, check my playlist on UX Process and Methods as it covers some points.

Hope it helps; keep on rocking!

Thanks

    Vy"

The thank you note I received:

"Thanks, this is exactly what I was after. I'll try to study it in depth going forward!"

… And a follow up after some time:

"Hey V,

    I just wanted to reach out and thank you again. The NNG article was great and helped me out a lot, especially to use as an example when talking to the product managers.

Now I have a dilemma, what are your thoughts on personas? I know I need to do them, but I don't get the point.

Thanks,

    BT"

Did you notice how that last message ended with a simple, concise question? Do you think I replied with an answer? Of course I did. I also asked them a further question to find out more about their exact situation.

This junior designer reached out respectfully and made sure to follow up to get permission for future communication. Because of this, I did reply several times after and unintentionally told them to "let me know how that goes". That's an unmistakable signal that it's ok to keep in touch.

∞

HOW TO ALIENATE A POTENTIAL MENTOR

Through my own experience advising designers and researchers, I've noticed a few nasty "tools" and tactics that, surprisingly, many developing designers use.

Leave nasty, backhanded compliments or outright personal hate

While this one seems like an obvious thing not to do, unfortunately in my experience it's not that rare. Because of the relatively anonymous nature of the Internet, people feel less accountable for their actions than they should be. They can do stupid things knowing there's no consequence. The hateful comments are few, but any person who puts themselves out there will receive them.

For example, I received a comment saying *"Your videos suck, you don't know what you're talking about..."*. A few weeks later, that same commenter emailed me politely to ask for UX career advice. Their name sounded familiar and, lo and behold, when I checked my comments it was the same person.

While most of you won't even consider going as far as crapping on someone else's work, make sure not to sabotage your chances of forming a relationship that could lead to mentorship. It's safe to say that this keyboard warrior did not get my mentorship or advice.

Ask vague or open-ended questions

People often share too much information that is hard to scan for someone who has minimal spare time. Sometimes I get pages worth of material that would require a response that's the depth of an article or a book.

However, don't be too vague either. The less specific you are in the reach out, the less likely you are to get a response. I receive "hey" messages without any context and I can't remember the last time I replied to any of them - there is just no time to chat. Always keep it concise, always get to the point. Maybe after you've developed a relationship, they can help you with something larger.

Expect an instant reply

It's practically impossible to reply to every single email, especially in a timely manner. For example, I have a dedicated one day every two weeks to respond to my viewers and email senders. This means you'll have to be patient after you send off that message.

The worst you can do is to follow up angrily, saying something passive-aggressive like, "*you could at least send me a NO!*" This is one way to guarantee losing access to advice or a mentorship opportunity.

Expecting anything at all

Let's face it: no one owes you anything. Like many relationships and growth opportunities, you'll need to reach out to enough people to find a good working relationship match. Some people you might think would be a great mentor might be too busy at that point in their lives, others not open or confident enough to help you out. The best you can do to increase the chances of finding a mentor is to continuously and without expectations reach out to people until you find one.

Note that people will never forget the nasty few who, for whatever reason, decide to use relative anonymity as a medium for hatred. Don't forget that the design world is very small, and the UX community is even smaller. **Be more human: respectful, humble and unassuming.**

Make sure to immediately reach out to people who are more experienced than you. Don't expect instant mentorship, but reach out to introduce yourself and why this person matters to you, add value, ask questions and see if you can develop trust over time to create an organically and mutually beneficial mentor-mentee relationship.

The best mentors you'll have won't be someone you'd call a mentor at the time but perhaps only in hindsight.

FAQS

Who is the right person to mentor you?

Anyone who you look up to and who is where you want to be. It will help if you look for a mentor who's not too senior compared to you. If you're just starting out, you could go as low as a junior or as high as a senior or lead designer.

Make sure that the people you look up to are in the right place: geographically, in terms of focus (UI or Product or UX or Service design or...), in the right type of organisation, have the right work experience in terms of placement role (contract, permanent, freelance...) and other factors.

What about the recent boom of mentorship platforms and communities that link design mentors with mentees?

In short, they are a great option if you are picky enough. But you must know what is proper mentorship and what is just community advice. What puts me off from those platforms is the transactional nature of mentorship. Some require rigidity, which is the polar opposite of forming the long-lasting mentor-mentee relationship I described before.

However, if you can link up with the right person, it can save you a lot of worries, as the mentor will probably already be in the right mindset to welcome you and give you advice. Just don't make it transactional.

I found a mentor who is charging $$$/hour – is it worth it?

You found a career coach, not a mentor. If you have specific issues you want to address, they might be a good option, but I wouldn't call that mentorship. True mentorship is not transactional in any way and is built on top of mutual respect and trust.

For example, a mentor will want to give back to the community or see something in you and want to help you out regardless of what's in it for them. Likewise, from your side, you'll want to learn and demonstrate your gratitude by actioning their advice.

∞

FIND YOUR DESIGN COMMUNITY

While finding mentors is a challenging effort that needs to be consistently worked on, joining existing communities is something you can do immediately, online or in person. You can quickly benefit from your membership and participation.

ONLINE COMMUNITIES

If you haven't engaged in conversations on social networks yet, start now. You have almost every experienced UX designer available at the click of a button. You can follow, engage in discussions and otherwise reach out with queries using the advice I shared above, or passively learn from them by shadowing remotely.

I'd suggest engaging with people who are slightly ahead of you but not too far ahead career-wise. For example, pros who "have made it a long time ago" will have very little time to focus on answering every question or participating in every discussion.

Meanwhile, an only slightly more advanced UX peer might be glad to spend a few minutes answering your questions or pointing you in the right direction based on their own, still recent, experience.

Generally speaking, a mid-weight designer might give you techniques, methods and prototyping tool advice, while more senior designers (who after years of hard work are more strategically minded) might tell you that tools don't matter at all and instead will advise you on interpersonal skills. Ultimately, both advice sources are extremely valuable.

As a rule of thumb, you should aim to set achievable goals that are far enough to be a stretch, but also achievable within months or a couple of years at most. I recommend to connect with people who are in the ballpark of your goal - so you get topical advice that can help you get to that next step.

Example community platforms

One of my favourite communities, Quora, is a platform where you can ask questions and give answers. It doesn't matter if you choose to do so there or on another platform – you should be firing questions left and right. And, if you do get a response, engage with the comments to get even more insights and to foster a connection.

Here's a simple example: a person asked me a question, which I was more than happy to answer. When they followed up with a matter related to it, we had a good chat right afterwards.

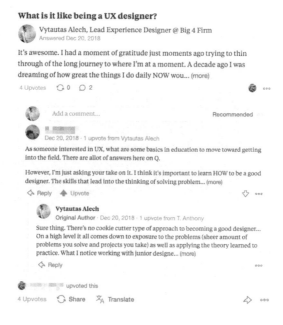

This might seem like a trivial engagement, but if you ask questions and communicate with more experienced designers, you will start thinking more like them. The new ways of thinking will allow you to make more robust connections in UX skills and knowledge and help you become a more confident designer.

Another practical example of a community you can immediately join without feeling like an impostor is the **Design Squad**. Sometime back, I created a simple Discord server where people like yourself could freely connect, request advice, share learnings, helpful material and tools, etc.

Design squad

It's another way to become part of a network in a few clicks. Go to https://bit.ly/designsquadux to join today.

HOW TO GET STARTED AND MAKE THE MOST OUT OF ONLINE COMMUNITIES

At a minimum, you should join and start discussions on social media communities: Twitter chats, Quora spaces and questions, Facebook groups, YouTube channel comments and community spaces or dedicated forums and blogs.

If you have an issue, you should first google for what other designers have to say about it. Once the problem at hand becomes clearer, find a discussion so that you can exchange information to take the learning further.

I'd recommend, at a minimum, being actively involved in at least one major social network. Ideally, pick a place where designers you'd like to hear from actively engage.

Ensure that each engagement is meaningful, thought out, and is not asking anyone for too much. However, do not hesitate to challenge yourself and others in discussions.

You'll probably be more wrong than right about UX and research and that's fine because you're still growing into the field. Being wrong is exactly how you can identify gaps and learn from people who are just a bit more advanced than you are.

∞

SOCIAL COMMUNITIES AND MEET-UPS

I've put online and remote communities as the first option for a reason. Depending on when you're reading this, social interaction might be even more challenging to come by. I'm typing this in the middle of the Covid-19 pandemic, where social events of any sort have become history.

Regardless of the circumstances, what's unlikely to change is the ease of use, proximity, cost efficiency and other factors that make remote communities so much more viable. However, if the time comes when we can gather again in person, there is no better way to connect.

As a growing designer (from entry to lead seniority level), I made a personal challenge to attend at least one meet-up a week. Granted, I lived in London which was booming with communities. Your situation might be the opposite but that's ok. There still should be at least an occasional get-together within the local or reachable tech scene. If not, there's always digital communities to fall back on.

In my case, when there weren't any UX related in-person events, I attended those for developers or marketers. It all expanded my network, improved my social skills, and helped me understand which skills I excelled in and which I lacked.

This is also why I wanted to add this section: you should attempt to commit to regular outreach to the broader design community. Perhaps you live in a smaller town, or there's no tech hub to make this happen – start one yourself.

Being part of a community and staying connected will provide the extra boost you need to keep on going.

∞

LEARN UX SKILLS FASTER

If you're reading this book, you probably want to learn UX skills faster. Everyone does. But not everyone wants it for the right reasons. Sometimes people say 'work smarter, not harder' but they say it because they don't want to work hard (or at all), not because they want to be more efficient.

In reality, if you want to get into UX, you'll need to work smart AND hard. The intelligent part is about employing the right tools and focusing on the right skills to foster; the hard part is putting in consistent effort to improve.

There's at least a couple of simple learning methods that, in combination, can help you learn smarter. If either of these methods stand out to you, I recommend that you seek out the original books about them as they'll go into more depth than I can on these few pages.

$$\infty$$

THE KAIZEN 1% PRINCIPLE

If you have a growth mindset, you already know that you should prepare for challenges (those days when you won't feel like learning new things or when external circumstances work against you). Those happen but you shouldn't allow them to break your habit of learning about UX consistently (ideally daily). Anticipating these challenges is the premise of the Kaizen 1% principle that describes the bare minimum effective measure to ensure continuous improvement.

While Kaizen has Japanese word origins and means good change, the original outline for Kaizen usage in self-improvement was documented by business management theorists during the US depression era. Then, a gradual and consistent progress of 1% was shown to accumulate to substantial yearly outcomes:

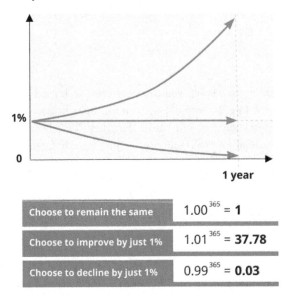

Improvement or decline?

Choose to remain the same	$1.00^{365} = 1$
Choose to improve by just 1%	$1.01^{365} = 37.78$
Choose to decline by just 1%	$0.99^{365} = 0.03$

Applying the same principle to your learning, you don't need to try to be 2x better every single day of every month. You just need to show up daily to learn about UX (e.g., even if all you do is a single small lesson from a course, or an article or a video on a specific subject). This will still keep you moving on an upward trajectory.

In the words of author James Altucher: "*Improve a little each day. It compounds. When 1% compounds every day, it doubles every 72 days, not every 100 days. Compounding tiny excellence is what creates big excellence.*"[1].

Simply put: you can become 2x better at any skill every 72 days.

The catch is that you must commit to establishing the habits to do this regardless of circumstances. Consistency matters a lot more than how much you take in at one time. If you dabble in UX occasionally, whenever you feel like it, it won't benefit you in the long run even if you go all in when you do dabble.

Instead, if you take in bite-sized pieces every single day, you will find growth before you know it. **What you do every day matters far more than what you do every once in a while.** You don't have to feel intimidated that you can't learn everything in one day!

The Kaizen principle has been the most transformative for my own personal and career development. It affected how I approach each habit-forming and learning effort.

Every junior UX designer I've worked with who spent time to ensure they understand this method also reported much faster growth. In their minds, they are also moving ahead by doing less than what they usually would, but the improvements in skills are clear.

As Benjamin Franklin once put it: *"little strokes fell great oaks."*

THE DISSS METHOD

Alongside Kaizen 1%, one of the most powerful tools I've used to excel in UX was the DiSSS (or DS3) method developed by best-selling author and super-learner Tim Ferris [2]. He uses the DS3 to learn advanced skills, like foreign languages or playing an instrument, within days.

Whilst UX still takes years to master, applying DS3 and doing so diligently will shorten your journey into the field and beyond.

DS3 = Deconstruction + Selection + Sequencing + Stakes

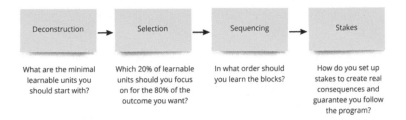

To start, you need to pool as many different UX related skills as possible. This is because you'll never learn 'UX'; you'll learn all the skills that make up its process. 'UX' is also too broad unless you want to know about UX on a high level, but not so much about its specific parts. If you've read this far, you're probably nodding along with me at this point.

For example, I'll take three random (but very important) skillsets I'd want to know well as a junior UX designer or researcher: qualitative research, experience mapping, information architecture. It would also be impossible to learn these three in isolation as you'd naturally touch other areas, but that's precisely why being picky and focussed will get you results in a shorter amount of time. In the end, you'll be able to connect the skills, activities and principles across more of the actionable parts of UX.

STEP 1: DECONSTRUCT ALL THAT YOU NEED TO LEARN

The first step of the DiSSS method is deconstruction. What are the minimal learnable units, the LEGO blocks, you should be starting with?

Every skill set you want to learn will have smaller building blocks and, for a lack of a better term, learning units. You can always divide it further until you arrive at a reasonably sized chunk that you can learn bit by bit.

Here's an example of learnable units for the above three skillsets:

Example skillset	Qualitative research	Experience mapping	Information architecture	...
	4 dimensions of user research	When to use different types of maps	Taxonomies	...
			Information hierarchy	
	When to use different types of methods	Mapping as-is and to-be experiences	Cognitive psychology	
	User interviews (planning, observation and facilitation)	Empathy maps	Data modelling	
		Journey maps	Cognitive maps	
Example learnable skill unit	Ethnographic field studies	Experience maps	Sitemaps	
	Usability studies (Moderated)	Service blueprints	...	
	Usability studies (Remote, moderated)	...		
	Participatory design			
	Desirability studies			
	...			

STEP 2: SELECT THE RIGHT LEARNING BLOCKS TO FOCUS ON

The selection step in the DiSSS requires one to use the Pareto efficiency principle of 80/20: Which 20% of the blocks should you focus on for 80% or more of the outcome you want?

If I'd be a junior, I'd probably look to improve my qualitative user research skills first (shortly after quant, if you haven't already). I could immediately apply the 80/20 to the research learnable skills units. For example, start with user interviews and moderated usability studies, covering the minimal needs to engage with users.

It's also what entry-level designers commonly use when entering the design field. When reviewing portfolios, I notice that even the most senior product designers sometimes only can do these two skills in terms of qualitative measures. User research! But don't get excited thinking these two skills are enough, as the UX capability of those designers is not up to par. For now, though, let's stick with user interviews and usability testing as our selective blocks.

Before going to the next step of sequencing, I'd recommend breaking the units into smaller blocks to create even more actionable baby steps. For example:

Example skillset	Qualitative research	Experience mapping	Information architecture	...
	4 dimensions of user research	When to use different types of maps	Taxonomies	...
			Information hierarchy	
	When to use different types of methods	Mapping as-is and to-be experiences	Cognitive psychology	
	User interviews (planning, observation and facilitation)	Empathy maps	Data modelling	
		Journey maps	Cognitive maps	
Example learnable skill unit	Ethnographic field studies	Experience maps	Sitemaps	
	Usability studies (Moderated)	Service blueprints	...	
	Usability studies (Remote, moderated)	...		
	Participatory design			
	Desirability studies			
	...			

Learnable skill unit	User interviews	Usability studies (moderated)	...
	Goals	Goals	...
	Hypotheses	Hypotheses	
	Planning	Planning	
	User recruitment	User recruitment	
	Incentives	Incentives	
	Scripting	Scripting	
Blocks	Conducting the interview	Moderation	
	Active listening	Active listening	
	Dialog provoking, open ended questions	Observation and notes	
		Data output	
	Probing and followup questions	Findings synthesis	
	Observation and notes	...	
	Data output		
	Findings synthesis		
	...		

Before you jump to the next step: some of the skills will have similar or identical blocks. For example, the following skills could apply to many different qualitative research methods: user recruitment, organising admin, incentives, assessment of the suitable candidates and picking the right number of them for your project.

You'll become a better UX designer the more of the overlapping skillset blocks you learn, as those skills will permeate.

STEP 3: SEQUENCE THE LEARNING BLOCKS

In what order should you learn the blocks?

Focusing on the right skills matters a lot; however, what also matters is to learn them in the right order. Above, I listed skills in my preferred order, as it follows close to the linear spread of blocks.

It forms a journey that you can quickly memorise to know which of the demonstrable actions you need to take next. This is also why the order and sequencing of the tiniest of skills matter so much.

If you're ever in doubt about the sequencing of the learnable skills - approach it like a user journey. Map out the end-to-end experience of actioning some skill. Let's take user interviews as an example; at a high level, doing this will include:

- **Planning**: setting goals, administering activities, scheduling research sessions, scripting etc.
- **Actioning**: conducting the research, observation, dialogue, observation, etc.
- **Reviewing**: data outputs, synthesis, playback, etc.

Naturally, you could also do another round of 80/20 to figure out which of the blocks will result in the most significant returns.

STEP 4: SET UP THE STAKES

How do you set up the stakes to create real consequences and guarantee you follow the learning?

This step is all about accountability. You could find a family member, friend, colleague, a stranger from a design community or a mentor to keep you accountable to your learning.

You can report to them as you learn and become more confident with different skills. The key is to pick a person who will not succumb to the empathy trap and let you slack off.

Use habit-forming accountability tools

There are behavioural science-based services that can make this step easier. For example, Tim Ferriss' primary recommendation for sticking with learning is the Stickk app[3].

It is a proven service where you commit to submitting a daily report on your progress towards a set goal. If you don't report or you miss your goal, the service takes a penalty amount (as set by you) from your account and donates it to an anti-charity.

For example, I've used *Stickk* while writing this book to develop a habit of showing up to work every single day. If I wouldn't show up at least once a day, the service would take $50 and donate them to a political party that no one wants to support. It works because you have to be honest with yourself and your commitment.

In around 2 years of writing this book, I haven't skipped a single day.

Get an accountability partner

While you can cheat with an app, as ultimately you're in charge and can opt-out anytime, it would be much harder to do the same with an actual person. Do you have someone in your life who can keep you in check and won't coddle you if things get messy? Someone who can tell you with a straight face that you aren't doing well enough? If not, get more people like this in your life.

We tend to steer away from people who have stricter standards or an abrasive attitude to life, but if you want to elevate the stakes for learning and getting into UX, this might just be the type of person you need. It's also why spouses, better halves, good friends, and other family members are lousy choices for accountability partners. They tend to be too supportive of your current state and unlikely to apply enough pressure.

It might be that your mentor could take that uncompromising role. (If they do, make sure that both your expectations are aligned.) Perhaps it could be a person from an online community who holds you accountable?

1. This concept has been also deconstructed in an easily applicable way by author James Clear in his book *Atomic Habits* - yet another read that's worth picking up.
2. While Tim Ferris' The 4-Hour Workweek book is not UX specific, it is focussed on helping people deconstruct and develop better habits in general. The real value of the book is in honing the meta skills that are required for you to learn more effectively.
3. Stickk is a platform that allows anyone to pick a challenge or make their own, set a timeframe and assign a monetary penalty if they don't check in daily about that challenge. Be careful though, as it can take time for you to form the habit of checking in. As with any behaviour forming effort, the penalty should be enough for you to care, but not too much to make you despise the challenge or the new behaviour.

DO YOU KNOW ENOUGH?

Pause for a brief moment and let me ask you this: What information in this book so far did you already know? What was your reaction to coming across it? You might feel like you already learnt a lot of this stuff from other resources. That's fine.

Reflecting on the things you already know is also an important part of growing into UX. Knowing what you know will help you identify adjacent knowledge that you can still acquire. On the flip-side it's almost impossible to know everything else that is out there to learn until you actually learn it.

WE DON'T KNOW WHAT WE DON'T KNOW

There are several stages of necessary growth to your development that you mustn't skip. The Dunning-Kruger effect illustrates them perfectly. If there's learning involved, you'll go through these stages whether you want to or not:

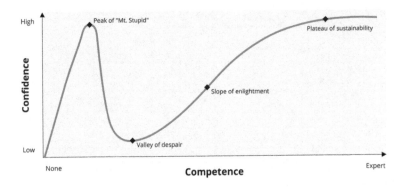

Understand that you have to go through these four phases in order to become competent in any skillset you will need to get into UX.

Mt. Stupid: this is where you'll find yourself when learning about a new skill. The majority of entry-level designers who do a bootcamp, take a course or read a book will end up on this hill. You gain a sudden boost in confidence, but in reality, you struggle to connect the theory with real-world scenarios. This is the danger zone, because if you're not self-aware you could stay there and fail to get into UX without understanding why.

The valley of despair: also known as the phase of feeling like an impostor because reality kicks in and you realise how complex the real world truly is. This is the longest stretch in anyone's journey to becoming a pro. It's also the perfect ground for learning and growth.

The slope of enlightenment: once the learning accumulates, you will develop real expertise in certain aspects of UX. This will take years to reach, and you should be ok with that.

The plateau of sustainability: being able to practice UX in commercial settings repetitively (and successfully) will develop your core, technical and interpersonal skills. This balance of considerable expertise usually takes decades to achieve.

WHY IS THIS IMPORTANT FOR YOU?

The majority of entry- to junior-level designers will get exposed to hundreds of data signals about what UX is and what it is not. Every researcher and designer will climb Mt. Stupid. Sadly, many will stay there for a long time if they aren't aware of where they are.

They will display the following symptoms:

- Stop doing the things that have helped them improve up to this point
- Get confused about what UX is, and as a result, be considered unqualified
- Get confused about what UX is, and as a result, get offered UI or visual design roles that can be learned faster
- Get stuck and frustrated because they can't move forward
- Are unsure about what's missing, they double down on skills that aren't UX which creates a brand-new lifecycle with its own phases and, as a result, prolongs their journey into UX
- Start blaming the industry and the more experienced designer for gatekeeping the UX field and not giving new entrants a chance

It's an obvious trap that can lead to weeks, months or years of frustration. If you actually knew enough, why wouldn't they have called you back for that interview?

Focus on the growth instead

Focussing on continuous growth will keep you curious, present and open to experiences. You will develop into a better designer.

Think about it this way: as a UX professional you need to be open to receiving raw ideas and delivering, in return, more refined outcomes that are worth paying for.

Putting your focus on an end goal – acquiring a certain amount of knowledge, a prescribed set of skills and experiences – instead of the journey will limit your curiosity, stifle collaboration, and will never allow you to reach the average or expert level in the field. Instead you should:

- **Choose yourself** – quite literally. I don't care if you did just a single course on UX, read a single article or book; it's time to choose yourself to put that knowledge into practice. Does it mean applying it professionally and getting paid? Not at first. But you must practice getting there. I'll unpack this concept later in the book, but for now, you must consider how you can get into the motions of choosing yourself. I'll cover this more in an upcoming chapter titled "Face the resistance and keep your head up".

- **Embrace challenges** and apply those UX skills you've learned to date (however roughly) to solve real problems.
- **See all efforts as a path to mastery**, focus on your growth and the journey because it is all that you will do until you arrive at your destination (breaking into the field).
- **Find lessons in all setbacks**. It doesn't matter if someone criticised you, put you down, ghosted you, or you otherwise failed. You must pick yourself back up and continue, rinse, repeat.

In more practical terms, when you encounter a method, framework, or even a research insight that you already know of, give more weight to it. **If you hear it twice, it must be worth paying more attention to.**

Don't dismiss it thinking you know better, as that weakens the knowledge you already acquired about it the first time. This behaviour is what keeps you on Mt. Stupid. Even if a concept that was once intimidating is now obvious to you, double down and learn even more about it. Keep your knowledge tank topped up.

Breaking into the field of UX and getting that first user experience job will not be as hard as becoming truly proficient at it. The latter takes time. That's why you must buckle down for the long haul and focus on the journey instead of collecting course attendance marks, diplomas, or other trivial checkbox exercises.

∞

CHAPTER 4

PRACTICE UX AND COLLECT THE EVIDENCE ALONG THE WAY

"Work, because it's not a hobby. You might not get paid for it, not today, but you approach it as a professional. The muse is not the point, excuses are avoided, and the work is why you are here."

SETH GODIN

Once you have the fundamental knowledge of UX and user research, it's time to start thinking about the practical application of said skills. This part is one of the most critical steps, as it's only practicing the theory that can validate the state of your skills.

A lot of entry and junior-level designers struggle to find the proper outlet to apply their UX skills. They don't know how to start a project or find a side gig that could get them good-enough case studies.

In this chapter, I'll share some of the simplest ways to get started with researching and producing user experiences. I'll give you tools and ideas for finding the right projects, documenting your activities with purpose and for finding ways to transform your developing UX skills into a consistent practice.

GAIN COMMERCIAL EXPERIENCE

"Champions behave like champions before they're champions: they have a winning standard of performance before they are winners."

BILL WALSH

In the first few chapters of this book, I listed a lack of commercial experience as one of the key reasons people can't get into UX. A lack of experience is a blanket statement that can cover many things, but what it really means is that the candidate is not qualified to take on the challenges in the job ad.

Employers look for 2-3 years of experience on average, even for the most junior-level jobs. But let me tell you why you shouldn't care about that requirement and why you should instead focus on what you can do now.

As a hiring manager I've reviewed hundreds (if not thousands) of applicants at various levels of seniority. I can tell you that the exact number of years of experience listed on the job description doesn't really matter. It's a filter made to weed out inexperienced designers who are still learning the ropes from those who have practiced their learnings.

Even for my own first proper UX role at a junior level, the job ad required at least 3 years of commercial experience. I had maybe a solid year of it, the rest I "collected" through self-directed and gig-based work.

As long as you can demonstrate *some* commercial experience in your portfolio, you will stand out from everyone else who can't even if they technically have more years of experience on paper.

When I talk to entry-level and junior designers about this, I can sense a universal confusion because nobody teaches how to get that commercial experience after the course, the book or the bootcamp is completed.

Designers leave courses knowing about user experience design and research activities but not knowing what to do next to action that knowledge. Understandably then, the leap between learning and getting the first role is one of the hardest steps.

What people think commercial experience means is the amount of years spent doing UX. Concrete, relevant examples of work in UX are, of course, one path forward, but there are other ways to gain this experience. Additionally, even if a candidate does have that type of experience, a hiring manager will still assess them to see if those years on the resume are backed up by learnings and experience.

You can gain adequate commercial experience without years of official work in a full-time job by doing the following:

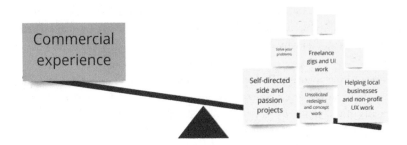

- **Running self-directed side and passion projects**
- **Solving problems with UX for real businesses** (even if you're unpaid at first)

- **Taking on freelance gigs**
- Most importantly, **maturing your portfolio and looking out for more complex work** to add to it over time

In other words, you can gain commercial experience by practising your UX skills and documenting the projects. But you have to do it right. For example, if you go out and do UI work without user research, your portfolio will be good enough for UI designer roles but not so much for UX.

This is where you'll need to invest your time so you can practice those newly learned skills. Ensure that the opportunities you do take on to build your profile are relevant and have concrete transferable skills that you can highlight during the application process.

WORK ON YOUR PORTFOLIO BEFORE YOU NEED IT

One of the biggest mistakes any junior can make is to hope that their portfolio will get better after getting their first gig, allowing them to capture quality UX work.

Your portfolio will undoubtedly improve after your first gig, but there's one huge obstacle: the harsh reality that you need to already have a strong portfolio to land that first gig.

It's important to understand how integral your work can be to a company's success, or failure. It can fail businesses if not done right[1]. While for most professions, a resume and references might be enough to get you in for an interview, UX research and design will require a solid portfolio because the company truly needs to trust that your work will not cause a catastrophe for them.

They need proof. Both social proof in the form of reviews and testimonials, and literal proof in the form of the projects showcased in your profile. That's why you need to collect enough evidence to prove that you know what you're doing.

I urge you to start working on your portfolio from day one of your journey, no matter how much or how little work experience you have. That's right. If you are currently taking a course – work on your portfolio; if you are studying – work on your portfolio; if you're working – work on your portfolio.

Until you get into UX, you should always be 1) working on a project, 2) looking for your next UX project, or 3) adding it to your portfolio.

It's surprising how many entry and junior-level designers learn the theory, make a case study or two and then wait to get picked for a job. That's not going to happen. You must commit to working on your case studies and your 'UX passport' long before you need it.

THE EVOLUTION OF YOUR PROJECT AND PORTFOLIO

But how do you start working on your portfolio before you need it? At the very start, you won't have enough material to show off your skills. And that's ok: almost every UX designer or researcher I know has started by working on at least a few side projects and passion projects.

I like to use this simple diagram to illustrate the evolution of your project work types:

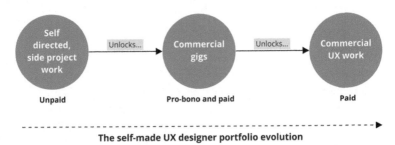

The self-made UX designer portfolio evolution

The key three steps in this flow are:
• **Step 1: Self-directed work:** side and passion projects
• **Step 2: Commercial gigs**: usually freelance work and inconsistent pro-bono and paid work that rarely covers end-to-end UX process. For example, someone might hire you to produce some UI designs only.
• **Step 3: Commercial UX work:** business gigs that could be unpaid

or paid depending on your experience, but allow you to cover user experience research and design appropriately.

All three can provide a relatively fail-proof environment for you to experiment with your skills. For example, in the side projects, you can do whatever you want in terms of scope, methods and activities. You are choosing what you want to work on, so you can very intentionally align the project and skills with the proper commercial UX work (step 3) you hope to obtain in the future.

With new, inconsistent commercial gigs (step 2) that might need more UI than UX expertise, you still have a lot of freedom to approach problems your way but you are also gaining the experience of working with another stakeholder in the form of a client or a business and gaining more transferable skills. In both cases, with enough repetition and some evidence, you can unlock even more work as you build out your portfolio.

To help you find work and create your projects, I'll now share some ideas you can focus on immediately. There are many issues in the world, and UX is the perfect discipline to understand and solve them.

---

1. In the past I've captured several BIG cases where lack of consideration for user centricity lead to disastrous situations; 3 worst UX failures in recent history: https://bit.ly/worstuxfailures; Citi's $900M loss over bad UX: https://bit.ly/citi900m; Blizzard's Diablo announcement failure: https://bit.ly/diabloimmortals

SIDE PROJECTS YOU CAN TURN INTO PORTFOLIO CASE STUDIES

What makes junior designers pick up the craft the quickest is to deconstruct their real-life experiences and then ideate on how they could improve them.

Don Norman's book *The Design of Everyday Things* asserts that you must start looking at the world around you as an imperfect place designed by people who have no idea what good UX looks like. This is by no means a complaint. Instead, it would be best if you took this as an opportunity to come in and develop outstanding user experiences.

You need to get into the habit of noticing and analysing UX in your own day-to-day. Over time, you'll develop a problem-solving muscle strong enough to immediately notice the noise between a product offering and the standards they meet or miss in terms of usability, desirability and meaning.

If you can reframe the way you look at the world around you, then the following few methods will help you start practising UX and doing experience design work.

SOLVE YOUR PROBLEMS

Personal experience often sparks creativity and innovation. If you look at top tech entrepreneurs and outstanding designers, most started out by addressing a pain point personal to them or to someone in their lives.

Too often, designers try to overreach: they want to start working on big projects right out of the (bootcamp) gate. As someone who is still learning UX design, you need to make an effort to apply and address your own issues, even if they seem simple. It means assessing which issues, activities and processes can be improved and then working on them.

I bet there are a tonne of experiences (digital or analogue) that you go through every day where you are the user. I bet it's not rare that you have a bad experience first-hand. So why not research, ideate and redesign it?

I recommend juniors to start by making a list of at least ten areas, actions or processes they encounter daily that aren't ideal. For example, maybe it's the drop-off process for parcels at your local post office. Perhaps it's that app you're using that needs a good re-evaluation; perhaps it's even a platform or service you used to learn about UX. Ironic, right?

Add a note of why and how they could be improved. Be as specific or as broad as you need to be. The aim here is to identify at least one area to which you can apply design thinking or UX principles, in order to make your own experience better.

UNSOLICITED REDESIGN AND CONCEPT WORK

On product design portfolio/showcase sites like Dribbble or Behance, you'll see a lot of conceptual and UI redesign work. There's the Facebook, Twitter and LinkedIn redesigns that look great at a first glance. There's also a tonne of weather apps, fintech dashboards showing random crypto fluctuations, and let's also not forget the healthcare GP appointment apps. These are just a few typical suspects for unsolicited concept work from UI and product designers.

What's missing in all of those cases is:

- User research (discovery, testing, amends)
- Ideation and prioritisation methods
- Information architecture
- Design rationale (usability heuristics, accessibility, and other UX principles)

… Among many other things.

The point I'm trying to draw here is that you can do conceptual project work but you must go beyond simple UI terms. All those missing activities and methods are what you need to start with. Then and if it's appropriate, add a UI layer on top.

Concept work is a good start when you can't think of any of your own problems you could solve for. To start with, why not pick a platform you use daily (social media, niche site, mobile app, etc.), then research and redesign the essential journeys based on your accumulated UX knowledge.

Scan the web, involve the users, test your hypotheses and prototypes with them. Then document everything, and you should come out with a good enough starter project.

PICK A PROJECT WHERE YOU HAVE ACCESS TO THE USERS

This point applies to every other idea I mention in this chapter. Many designers struggle to engage with users, especially on an informal project. As a result they might skip this step completely, hoping that their knowledge is enough to cover the research part.

This is a big mistake.

You always have access to customers and users – every single person is one. And so, not engaging with people or starting a side project in isolation is a recipe for a shallow project and case study, which won't be good enough for your portfolio.

The best UX design work (side projects, commercial, pro) will happen when you do it holistically and cover the research properly.

When designers complain that they don't have access to users, I always call out the following:

- **Friends, colleagues and acquaintances fit the user criteria**: everyone around you is a user of certain products and services. Observing them and asking them about their daily experience can give new insights into your project work. If they fit the specific user criteria, they can provide you with starter insights on which you can base your hypotheses and further research.
- **Online communities with plenty of quant and qual insights:** for example, Reddit, Discord, LinkedIn, Facebook, niche community forums (e.g. a train operator manager community on Facebook) and many more. All you need to do is search for keywords, browse the discussions and engage with good questions.
- **Platforms where you can engage with specific people and ask them whatever you want to find out**: the best example of this is Quora, but social networks like Twitter, LinkedIn, and others can provide this as well. You might just need to work harder to infiltrate those communities and DMs, earn people's trust, etc. Quora especially allows you to ask a specific question to specific people. For instance, you can ask: "What does your day look like as a train operator?" You would tag it with specific keywords like "train operator," "South West trains," "trains," etc. You can then select people who match your criteria from a suggested list and Quora will ping them to answer your question. Depending on the list of available people you might even be able to reach the train operators at South West trains to answer your question. If the question is good, you will get a response.
- **Follow-ups on Zoom with the same people if permission is granted:** If you do the above correctly, you will engage with people who will be willing to help you further. Some will do so

free of charge. All you'll need to do is appropriately arrange interviews, user testing, etc.

Naturally, a combination of all these research methods would make your eventual case study more informed and meaningful.

If you'd like to find out more about how to research without having direct access to the users, I documented a simple discovery exercise I have used to do this in the past: https://bit.ly/researchwithoutusers

However, it's worth noting that nothing will replace proper UX engagement and user research.

These suggestions should be used as the first step in your development. Ideally to spark more ideas, hypotheses that can inform appropriate user research to follow. Even if there are considerable ways to source insights that can unblock UX projects, as a UX designer make sure to always push the boundaries of the limits you face.

PARTICIPATE IN HACKATHONS

The previous points are all about finding an issue and solving it using UX as an individual; the next one is all about doing so with others. There are a lot of project-like ways to simulate team collaboration and other experience design dynamics.

Because of their goal-focussed, intensive nature, hackathons can be the intensive learning route to get that commercial experience. For some, it will be the perfect project simulator where they'll need to work quickly and with others, applying what they've learnt.

One key piece of advice if you want to go this route is to anticipate and plan for how much actual UX you can do before, during and after the event has passed. For example, you should come prepared with enough research or at least have high level secondary research that covers the theme of the event. Then during the event, you'd want to do just enough of fast paced research and design to help the team move forward. This doesn't have to be said, but after the event is completed you can validate and user test the solution to further improve it. Perhaps even make it an ongoing project that can eventually become a strong case study?

I have participated and represented UX in several hackathons throughout the years. One regret I have is not starting earlier, but hackathons were not nearly as available to participate in at that time. Today, you can find nearby hackathons online.

Make sure to stay humble and advocate for user needs. To help you prepare even better, check out this post where I documented a hackathon I helped run, adding a UX spin to it: https://bit. ly/hackathonsWithUX. In this post you'll find my process outline, setup and a few templates I used to cover the basic experience design needs quickly.

USE VAEXPERIENCE UX RESEARCH AND DESIGN PROJECT CHALLENGES

On my Youtube channel I've run several UX project challenges that helped people hone their research and design skills. These challenges help designers worldwide apply their existing UX skills to solve a problem given by yours truly.

For example, these are the latest challenges I've run:

- **A digital transformation of the US voting system**: where some designers researched the service end-to-end, while others redesigned mobile voting apps and considered how the current experience could be enhanced.
- **A redesign of the cancellation customer experience for a telecom operator**: where designers deconstructed the real-life scenario and touchpoints in a service that was ridden with

dark patterns. The results were an impressive set of UX case studies that covered new conversational UIs, service blueprints and many more projects that could enhance any growing designer's portfolio.

- **A redesign of a product that helps people find places to live within reasonable reach of the metropolitan areas:** where researchers and designers tried to revive a dead product that had become relevant with the sudden shift in customer behaviours in the UK housing market. The submissions varied from fully outlined case studies to in-progress discovery work.

While the majority of participants in these design challenges are already established professionals in junior, senior and lead roles, there are complete beginners as well.

These challenges are all-inclusive and open. Anyone (UX-er or otherwise) can join and do end-to-end UX projects or select just a part of user experience activities. What matters is the commitment to practice the skills and to challenge yourself to apply at least one new method to solve problems —all for the sake of learning and progressing further.

If you want to participate in one of these challenges, check out this playlist: https://bit.ly/UXchallenges. You'll find several videos with a variety of briefs, topics and issues to solve. I also provide online whiteboards with deconstructed business goals and user needs focussed briefs. All you have to do is pick one up and do the UX as it should be done.

The challenges on the channel are recurring and usually last weeks at a time. I designed them to help people learn new skills, push themselves outside of their everyday UX practice, and provide ideas and a playground for anyone to start and document a UX case study.

We've had several viewer submissions for every challenge so far. To see me walk through these and give feedback, select the videos with "Live review…" in the thumbnail or title.

∞

COMMERCIAL PROJECTS TO TURN INTO PORTFOLIO CASE STUDIES

Now that we've discussed some initial ways to get yourself out there and start building commercial experience, let's get into the details. If you haven't done any of the previously listed activities to come up with good side projects, stop here. Complete that step and come back when you have captured a case study's worth of material.

My biggest piece of advice for you throughout this whole book is to record everything you do and each project you engage in so that you can add it to your portfolio as evidence. For now, you will slowly build on top of your portfolio case studies and accumulate the evidence of your skills, which will eventually open new doors.

One of the ways to do so in a true professional environment is with clients you can engage immediately. These could be any commercial partner, for example, a barbershop around the corner, or your second cousin who needs a website, or a non-profit charity down the road.

It's unlikely that the first commercial partners you work with will want an actual UX process – they probably haven't even heard of it, or if they have, they might think it's just UI design. But here's the kick – make sure to do what they're looking for and to do good UX regardless.

Perhaps at first, they won't even need to see what you do behind the scenes. For example, user research, experience mapping, personas and other deliverable work can be done in the background, especially in the beginning.

It could be that you will get just a brief to make a flyer (which could be the start of more UX-related work to come), or they might give you a specific request, let's say to design an app. But what you do with that brief or how you choose to solve that problem is ultimately up to you. Like any other client, they will care about the quality of outcomes, not how you got there. You, however, are using their project to practice how to get there.

The following few examples are what I'd do today if I needed to restart my career from scratch:

REACH OUT TO LOCAL BUSINESS OWNERS AND OFFER YOUR SERVICES

To reiterate, I'd recommend this only to designers who already have some side projects under their belts. Local businesses will need to see work examples before trusting you to help them out. It doesn't even matter if it's paid or unpaid. This is another reminder that your portfolio outweighs your resume; you need to show, not tell, what you're capable of.

Before reaching out to businesses who might need a website, app, or another way to engage with their customers, put on a UX designer's hat and do your research. For example, you could do market research, competitive analyses, outline their key user groups, and more. You need to show relative understanding of the issues they face to connect with them quicker.

In a sense, this is a sales approach. As you hone your UX skills, you'll also need to develop sales and marketing skills, but this is a topic for a different book.

For now, just like with the non-profit work recommended before, I'd recommend sending out 2-3 emails each day to different businesses. Explain who you are, your goals, and state whether your services require payment as any business owner will primarily be commercially minded.

Try to be fair here, and consider if it's reasonable to ask for payment right away.

I started doing UI design work for free for several months until I collected enough evidence to charge professional fees. It's possible to bypass this but that might not work for all.

REACH OUT TO NON-PROFITS AND OFFER PRO-BONO SERVICES

Following from the previous point, don't get surprised if your first apprenticeship or shadowing opportunity is unpaid. I know this is one of those unpopular takes these days, but it's a fair one. As soon as you have some experience under your belt and a robust portfolio, you will be able to charge normal rates.

Look at it this way: you can only charge for work that results in significant returns for the business. If you aren't a pro yet, you're more of a liability than a value-add, so the company or person who takes you in is making an investment.

Perhaps they see potential in you to continue as a pro once you've learned the ropes. Maybe they want to give back, and the motivation is purely intrinsic. Either way, you shouldn't expect to be rewarded financially right away. I always recommend that you dedicate time to learning instead of going out for the money right away. Your lifetime earning potential will be higher in the long run if you take your time at first.

Don't take this the wrong way, I've been there myself. While studying, I had a shadowing opportunity and did so free of charge for several months. Then I started contributing and adding value, so it was a no brainer for the company to start paying me. You have to contribute value before you are rewarded for that value.

START CHARGING BUSINESSES YOU'VE HELPED IN THE PAST

This option might be best for you if you have already done some professional, not-for-profit or freelance work. You need either a track record or sound enough evidence to convince people to pay for your services.

However, if you have delivered value previously, you should be able to reach out to them asking for paid opportunities. At the very least, they might give you a referral to someone who could benefit from your help. Alternatively, the next time an opportunity presents itself, they will think of you and know who to contact.

Juniors who decide to build themselves up through free labor might feel uncomfortable or weird about asking to be paid, especially at a high enough rate. That's fine. Impostor syndrome can rear its head anytime. I've been there countless times and never met a designer who hasn't felt it at some point. I urge you to ignore it and ask for compensation anyway.

After you've been working for free for a while and have experience under your belt, your work should be valued for what it's worth. You can start your rates low and increase them slowly over time. You have to take that leap towards exchanging your services for money, especially if there's a considerable amount of value you can add to that business. Good UX can increase the revenue of a business exponentially, and you should be compensated for that improvement.

Make sure to reach out to every business or non-profit you've helped to date with a simple thank you note. If they respond and are curious to hear from you – that's fantastic. Ask about any opportunities they might have in the future.

Alternatively, you can always ask if they know anyone who would benefit from your skills. It's as effortless as that; you need to proactively and consistently reach out. Put the idea in their minds and it will eventually lead to opportunities.

∞

OFFER SERVICES IN AN ONLINE DIGITAL MARKETPLACE

Yet another way to work on your skills and capture evidence is to run micro gigs via online digital marketplaces. While most of these gigs will be specific task-based activities, doing them can still give you extra experience and the ability to practice on real commercial problems.

Most of the work here is in the realm of visual or UI design. People who use marketplaces to get design help are looking for quick deliverables rather than for in-depth UX. It's up to you to decide how you'll arrive at that UI design.

As before, I'd recommend researching, engaging with users (however relative or remote) and applying deeper UX methods to outline the experience before jumping into product design. Make the most of the freelancing gigs you get, even if they're not exactly what you want to be working on.

These gigs might also provide some funding to sustain you while you apply for UX positions. However, this is not guaranteed. The open marketplaces, especially for design, are very competitive where the lowest price, the best looking portfolio and the highest-rated designers usually get the work. Some common digital marketplaces are: *99 design, Fiverr, Upwork, Creative Market, Design Crowd, Toptal,* and many others.

Even if you are in a good place and don't need more projects or additional income, freelancing can be a great playground to test your skills and to keep improving while building up commercial experience.

You will also build up reviews and testimonials that can be useful in acquiring a job. For example, I used reviews from happy clients to add to my otherwise very empty resume when trying to get my first professional role in the industry.

∞

DOCUMENT THE EVIDENCE ALONG THE WAY

I get many requests to make a step-by-step tutorial for making the perfect case study. The problem is that such a thing doesn't exist: there's no cookie-cutter approach that works for every problem.

Instead, in the following few chapters I'll share some go-to heuristics to follow when making a case study. For now, the critical part is to start working on your case study at the point of starting the project. Or ideally, even earlier.

The real reason you might be struggling to come up with case studies is that you document the work after the projects are long done. Most people will wait to start working on their portfolio until they need to apply for a job. The longer you leave this essential process, the less likely you are to craft a compelling story.

THINK ABOUT OUTCOMES TO MAKE BETTER DECISIONS

For every project you start (whether it's personal or commercial), you need to always think about the impact and outcomes ahead of time.

Based on the Project Logic Model[1], I like to use the following mental model to support day-to-day UX decisions:

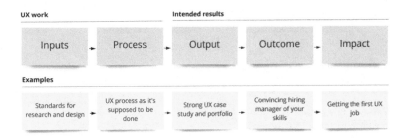

In the example above, if we reverse the model and start with the impact ('Getting the first UX job') as the primary goal, we can then work backwards to see that the inputs required include needing to have high standards for following the UX process properly.

There's a few big reasons to approach each project like this:

- **Thinking about impact and outcomes** will make you use more appropriate UX methods, as you'll need to think about the next steps and tools more carefully. It's kind of like when you know that someone will review your work; you'll pay more attention to ensure that it's spot-on.
- **Consistency and better methods will result in quality**. When I first started designing, I often used the saying 'you're only as good of a UX designer as your last project'. It helped me do the right thing. Every case you work on has to be just a bit better than the previous one for you to progress. If you think this way, you will always be reaching for something better and therefore produce quality on every project.
- In doing so, **your natural excitement and motivation levels will be much higher than** if you were just ploughing through the work. If you keep it in the back of your mind that you're doing this work to produce a better case study, you'll give your work another purpose that could save you from the burnout that's typical in the design field. When the times get tough (and they will), you'll have a personal goal that will keep you moving forward.
- Setting yourself up so that every decision you make is directly linking to the endgame makes you more likely to succeed and achieve **your goal of getting into UX**.

A common mistake with junior portfolios is that they rely on artefacts and deliverables alone to get to their goal of having a case study instead of thinking more holistically. A case study is also often their goal for each and every project. However that's a backwards approach to UX.

Instead, you should use mental models like the one on the previous page to clearly guide your decisions. Using impact as you starting point will start a knock-on effect that will force you to pick better methods, tools, activities and keep UX standards high.

DOCUMENT EVERY STEP

Once you get into the right mindset, you'll also need to think about capturing all the relevant artefacts, snippets, themes, photos, deliverables to save and store for later use.

Nothing works better than coming up with a solid structure you can rely on no matter the project. **That structure has to 1) support UX project workflow and 2) provide a structure that can be easily tapped into when you make your case studies.** As a practical example, in one of my videos (https://bit.ly/ documentingUX), I covered how I structure my project work.

The structure I use enables me to refresh my portfolio whenever I need to do so. It also supports the management of project assets as required throughout the project. Make sure to watch the video to understand the rationale behind structuring your projects in this way. It looks something like this:

1. Project type, title, year and any other identifier.
I split my projects into conceptual work, chargeable client work, and business development work (BD), sitting somewhere between the first two.

2. UX phases or steps in chronological order.
Folders labeled with a 0 before the name are admin work. The numbers from 1 and on are the actual UX phases. I start with pre-project assets such as branding, design, requirements, data, previous research and anything else my team or I could pick up to get started. The same applies to UX team management which, in your case, might not be relevant at all. After that are the key folders where the majority of assets live.

3. Specific milestone segments to each phase.
To recall information effortlessly, I document workshops or key milestone events. I've got inception, planning as 0's as they are more of the admin activities for the discovery, while the numbers 1-3 outline essential workshop, user research, and final deliverables (most likely research decks for playbacks to the business).

This simple system works pretty well as long as you maintain the focus on consistently documenting your process. Once the project finishes, you can extract the relevant themes and pull together a compelling story for your case studies.

THE ABC

The ABC stands for Always be capturing[2]. Google Ventures recommend this tool for use during workshops to quickly synthesise what's being said, however I think it can be applied more broadly and across different UX activities. For example, the ABC method can help you document your project work the right way.

The single best action any new designer or researcher can take is to always keep a notepad and pen on hand. The second one is to capture every insight their ears and eyes pick up. However menial it might seem at the moment. This is my number one recommendation to every junior who joins my teams and wants to become a more effective UX designer.

There are a lot of reasons why it's helpful:

1. In the beginning, junior designers lack confidence in their skills and, in specific or new environments, they can retreat inwardly. **Jotting down notes can relieve the pressure of facing many different emotions and inputs at once.**

2. **The ABC method can almost always spark you to ask followup questions**, which is an essential skill in UX research, facilitation and other activities.

3. **Jotting things down can enhance recall.** While you ABC what's going on around you, you'll be able to swiftly assess what is helpful to keep and what isn't even before you sit down to synthesise it.

4. **Capture as much information as you can during the research, workshops, and other sessions, even if it seems like it's too much.** While most of it might not be useful, it's better having to trim down than to lack insights or have to extend the research effort.

Capturing information is not just about writing stuff down. You can take photos of the day-to-day ethnographic scenarios, user environment, workshop boards, and other settings. You could also record audio and transcribe the information later as appropriate. Make sure to get written permission where necessary.

The ABC method is a simple, three-letter approach that can transform an observer into a contributor. Keep this in mind the next time you feel out of place or if you think you don't have enough material to put into your case studies after the project is done.

∞

FAQS

What if I use Figma, Miro, Mural or any other cloud-based software to store my project files?

Great – the same principles apply, minus the folder structure. My personal favourite is Miro. It works wonders because of its flexible layout that can accommodate any artefacts (documents, experience maps, etc.) you use as a researcher or designer.

How much information should I be documenting for later case study work?

You should capture as much as you can without infringing on NDAs or any other data privacy agreements.

Your first goal should be to document items for immediate project work, to inform decisions and allow you to move to the next phase. As long as you capture enough for that and don't lose any valuable artefacts, there shouldn't be any gaps.

---

1. Quoting W.K. Kellogg Foundation Evaluation Handbook (1998): "This model provides a road map of your program, highlighting how it is expected to work, what activities need to come before others, and how desired outcomes are achieved"
2. As a growing designer the ABC: "Always be capturing" is a fantastic tool that you should employ all the time. You can find out more about in Sprint: How to Solve Big Problems and Test New Ideas in Just Five Days book by Jake Knapp or this Google Ventures article: https://bit.ly/AlwaysbeCapturing

FACE THE RESISTANCE AND KEEP YOUR HEAD UP

The biggest generator of long-term results is learning to do things when you don't feel like doing them. Discipline is more reliable than motivation.

SHANE PARISH

Shane hit the nail on the head here because your journey into UX is going to take time. Due to various obstacles, you'll find hours, days, and weeks where you won't feel like doing anything to progress in UX. Sometimes you might feel stuck; other times you might lack motivation.

Learning UX, just like any other super complex discipline, requires precisely that – discipline. You need to trust the process of UX and do it continuously until it becomes second nature. Relying on motivation to get things done is a recipe for failure. And to be frank, feeling motivated alone won't get you into UX design.

Steven Pressfield, the author of the must-read book *Do the Work* describes the constant battle between us and progress as resistance:

"Resistance cannot be seen, touched, heard, or smelled. But it can be felt. We experience it as an energy field radiating from a work-in-potential. It's a repelling force. It's negative. Its aim is to shove us away, distract us, prevent us

from doing our work. … Rule of thumb: The more important a call or action is to our soul's evolution, the more Resistance we will feel."

Resistance is the opposing force that tells you that you aren't worthy or ready. It's what makes you feel like now is not the right time to do something you should be doing.

Resistance is that annoying natural force that keeps most of us procrastinating or worse - blocked. Only those who challenge the notion and show up anyway excel.

How learning and getting into UX appears:

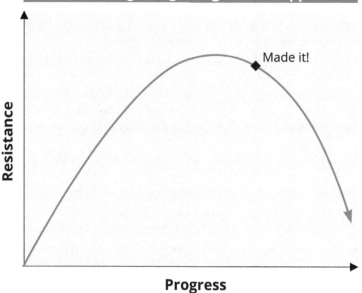

Made it!

Resistance

Progress

How it really is:

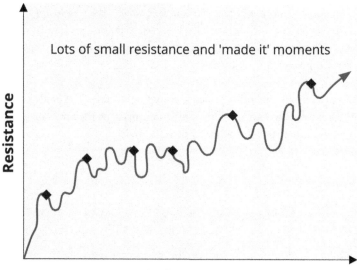

Lots of small resistance and 'made it' moments

Resistance

Progress

Knowing this, you shouldn't wait for motivation or inspiration to get going. Instead, you must be disciplined and do the work anyway. One thing will lead to another and with enough repetition, you can get to a state of flow, which people often compare to feeling engaged or motivated but in a more sustainable way. The secret is to push past those initial signs of resistance until they fade.

The following mental frameworks can make overcoming resistance a tad easier. I always share them with junior designers especially.

CHOOSE DISCIPLINE OVER MOTIVATION

Books on leadership from the former SEAL commanding officer Jocko Willink made me 10x the leader I was before reading them.

You don't have to read his books unless you want to supercharge your leadership skills early. However, there is one concept he talks about that can transform how well you learn and perform now. He calls it **extreme ownership**. What this means in practical terms is choosing to use discipline and discomfort to your advantage.

Jocko puts it simply as *"Discipline equals freedom"*. The way to apply this is to make a commitment to practice UX every day for a specific amount of time and to do so. Then the rest of your time you can freely spend on leisure, other activities and goals.

Another way to apply this principle would be to target the hardest things on the to-do list first. Do the hard things first (which are usually what needs attention the most anyway) then feel relief and freedom for the rest of the day.

CHOOSE LONG-TERM IMPACT OVER SHORT-TERM OUTCOMES

Thinking long-term and ignoring the short-term outcomes is by far the hardest thing to do. It requires you to look beyond immediate needs and sacrifice comfort.

As a practical example, I often get designers reaching out to me wanting to apply for UX positions on one of my design teams. However, when I ask if they can share their portfolio with me, their responses are often along the lines of "*still working on it*" or "*I'll be done with it in the next two weeks*".

Time passes and I still get nothing. Sometimes I even follow up and the response I get is filled with excuses. They naturally didn't go above and beyond to practice UX craft, collect the evidence, and all the other stuff you know by now.

I know how hard it is to work on UX case studies and portfolios when there's no immediate reward. But it's the choice you must make regardless of the resistance. No one will do it for you - even if you could afford to outsource it, you can't get someone else to write about your own experience on a project.

Don't rely on immediate gratification or external stimuli to make you feel like doing things. Think about that future self – the vision board I asked you to make in the first few chapters. You must work hard today to make that vision tomorrow's reality.

∞

CHOOSE TO MAKE TIME

> "*When you say 'I don't have time', what you are really saying is that it's not a priority. Because if it would be a priority you would make the time to do it. That's just how life works...*"
>
> NAVAL RAVIKANT

In your day to day, you'll have plenty of reasons and activities that will distract you from working on your dreams. There's always going to be TV shows to catch up on, a drink to have with a friend or any other leisurely thing that is easier to do than work on UX. It's up to you to use that extra hour in the day to learn and practice instead.

To better illustrate the importance of carving out time, let's compare these two cases: 1) someone who works on becoming a UX designer only when they feel like it, versus 2) someone who allocates a solid block of time, daily, or weekly. Who do you think will have a better set of skills and the evidence needed to break into UX?

The first case doesn't stand a chance in a market saturated with candidates who have limited experience. A lot of entry-level designers look for short-cuts, so their UX knowledge and evidence is shallow. **Any person who invests extra effort will immediately stand out from the crowd of applicants.** The second case is rarer than you might think but they are the ones who get invited to interviews and hired!

Make time for UX by sacrificing leisure time. Carve out what you can: for some that's 15 minutes a day, for others it's 45 or more. Over time, these small investments will turn into projects, then case studies and finally they will accumulate into a killer UX portfolio.

The majority of people who have gotten into UX or got a better offer were the ones who had strong side project case studies. That's precisely why an hour spent learning and practicing today can mean all the difference tomorrow, even if you don't feel like it or even if the conditions in your life are against you.

Prioritise UX and make time.

∞

CHOOSE YOURSELF

The Spotlight Effect is a recurring theme in studies of the human psychology[1]. It states that we go through our lives thinking that we are the main character in our film and that everyone else is a supporting character. In reality, we are also an extra to someone else's story.

To choose yourself might sound like more of the same individualism that would make you focus even more on YOU, however this is a very different concept as explained by author James Altucher. Built on top of the spotlight effect and applied to the UX industry, it means that no one is going to come out of the blue and ask you to be a UX designer.

You must choose yourself to be a UX designer. Choose yourself by working hard, persevering, learning, practicing, documenting the process and pulling together the evidence. And you will get into the UX industry.

Choosing yourself is a straightforward mindset that you must employ to make any significant commitment. It means not waiting for the perfect mood, environment or **permission** to be a UX designer. If permission is what you feel you need, you already have it by picking up this book.

Because resistance will never go away, you have to practice these methods until they become habits. With enough repetition of showing up, regardless of how you feel or what the resistance tells you, you will force a mindset shift and become a continuous learner.

Over time, you will start to love the nitty-gritty part of the UX world that lies beneath the glossy surface. If you take away just one message from this book – make it this part. **Envision your end goal. Choose yourself. Work hard in small amounts every day. And you will succeed.**

---

1. *The spotlight effect in social judgment: an egocentric bias in estimates of the salience of one's own actions and appearance*; T Gilovich 1, V H Medvec, K Savitsky, 2000: https://bit.ly/SpotlightEffect

CHAPTER 5

DEMONSTRATE THE EVIDENCE

Your portfolio is your passport to UX jobs

YOURS TRULY

I recently started using the phrase 'your portfolio is your passport' to emphasise the importance of having a strong showcase of your work.

Unless you travel for a living, your UX portfolio is more valuable than your actual passport. While the latter allows you to go places, the former will either open doors to employment or keep them shut.

You might already have a portfolio. Perhaps you're even happy with it, but there's always room for improvement. I've reviewed countless portfolios in the last decade trying to fill roles in UX, product design and user research, and almost all applicant portfolios out there are subpar. In my experience out of every 10 people I advise, 9 could benefit from a massive overhaul of how they present themselves and their work to hiring managers.

Naturally, creating a killer UX portfolio is not an easy task. Even if you already followed the steps I highlighted before, there are some key bits that juniors tend to overlook.

For example, can you tell a compelling story with the assets you've documented and collected to date? How about the content itself: is it more than a collection of floating UI mockups, a few screenshots, personas, experience maps or flows? Does it all tie in well together to engage the audience and help them make a hiring decision?

Using the information in the following chapters will help you cover these issues. If you follow my advice diligently, the next (or the very first) version of your UX portfolio will have employers asking for more.

THE UX PORTFOLIO DO'S AND DON'TS

As humans we are extremely risk averse. We avoid risk at all costs[1]. This is why a lot of tips, tricks, rules and religious doctrines are phrased in the negative form, using a "don't", "you shall not" and other similar expressions. The is because it's easier to not do something, as it feels more important. There's a name for this concept – *via negativa*[2].

I'll use this same concept and share my portfolio advice as a list of DON'Ts:

- **DON'T showcase a mixture of branding, UI, research, illustration, video, UX work in one portfolio**. Whatever work you put in your portfolio acts as a signal that you want to do more of that work in the future opportunities. While bunching variety of different work examples is acceptable for agency and jack-of-all-trades roles, it might not be the message you want to tell to all consumers of your portfolio.
- **DON'T showcase as many case studies as possible**. You're wasting the hiring manager's time as they now have to scan the whole portfolio to filter out the work most relevant to the role you're applying for.
- **DON'T write a novel**: As your portfolio user, I have 5-10mins tops to review and decide if it's worth inviting you for a chat. Make sure that all your case studies are squeaky clean,

snappy and tell a story well enough. Some items, like research studies, are naturally longer form but even these could be goal-driven and engaging so you don't lose the user's attention.

- **DON'T throw in random deliverable screenshots and examples without tying them into a cohesive story**. This signals inattentiveness, lack of care or laziness. None of these are good attributes for any profession, especially UX.

- **DON'T use inauthentic or fabricated material**, or material that does not belong to you. Portfolios often contain stock imagery of post-it notes, people at work, etc. If the recruiter doesn't notice this, the hiring manager will. Trust me, we know what Unsplash is.

- **DON'T fake your introductions and credentials**. If you introduce yourself as a senior or lead designer, but your resume shows the opposite, this won't look good. Presenting yourself as simply a UX designer won't hurt your application. As I've mentioned, it's all about the portfolio you can show them, not the seniority on your resume.

- **DON'T forget to list out any of the following information in an overview**: project timeframes, responsibilities, team setup, ways of working and other bits related to project management.

- **DON'T forget to credit other people involved in the project**. While you don't have to credit anyone, if you do so, it does give you extra points as it acts as evidence for the statements that you worked with a wider team. UX is a team sport (I'll elaborate on this in chapter VII: Collaborate), and so presenting your work as a team work will always make you look like a more grounded and effective designer.

- **DON'T use UI snapshots on Dribbble or other networking platform sites to apply for a UX role**. This is a big no that baffles me every time. I once also received an application that used Instagram as a portfolio site where the applicant posted their UI work samples. You need a real portfolio.

- **DON'T present your conceptual and commercial case studies in the same way**. Make it easier for your portfolio users to understand what sort of work they are looking at quickly. Nothing bothers me more than seeing a case study that looks 10/10 but then realising it was a conceptual case, and that fact wasn't mentioned anywhere. It's OK to include concept cases as long as you do your due diligence in UX research; just be upfront that they are concept cases so the hiring manager knows what they're looking at.

- **DON'T showcase work created under an NDA.** You need to look in the contract, NDA sheet or consult with the clients to understand what can be shared and in what capacity. While many designers resort to sharing work under password protection, this signals to the hiring manager that you might do the same with their client information after you leave. Make sure to consider all points and assess reputational and legal risk before using anything as portfolio material.

- **DON'T trash talk your previous clients in case studies.** It is surprisingly common for candidates to describe the challenge, business state or project itself in questionable ways. While some humour might help to illustrate specific points well, make sure it's tactful. In the end, you are not auditioning for a comedy special, and no one wants to work with someone who has a nasty attitude.

- **DON'T password protect case studies if you'll forget to share the password in your application**. This issue is widespread and annoying. The hiring manager then has to reach out to the recruiter, who then has to chase the candidate to provide the password. An additional point to consider is if protecting your work with a password sends the right message. Every time I type a password to access someone's UX work, that immediately signals that they are probably showcasing NDA material or material they shouldn't be sharing to begin with.

- **DON'T forget to cover project metrics and other tangible outcomes. Never fake results**. While it might not look suspicious on the portfolio itself, the hiring managers and design team will grill you if there's even a scent of fake information. It's a recipe for disaster. That's why a section for reflection is so important in each case study. You can openly list the shortcomings and what you'd do differently the next time you have a similar project in hand.

- **DON'T focus solely on the user experience.** While it is your sole job to advocate for user needs to deliver outstanding

solutions, another aspect of the job is ensuring that the
business that sponsored such effort also achieves its goals. The
worst portfolio owners only hint at or forget to mention
business goals, hypotheses, outcomes; the best designers cover
them holistically and highlight tangible results.

Did any of this surprise you? Are you guilty of any of these in your current
portfolio?

Consider how you could flip them around to your advantage. You can and
should reverse every negative here into the gain point. For example, the
point "*Don't showcase as many case studies as you possibly can*" can be
flipped into "*Showcase quality over quantity*". In other words, select just the
relevant case studies that match your client, their industry, design maturity, challenges and any other factors (which you should find out about by
researching online).

Now that we covered the DON'Ts, let's dig into a few things that can
make the material you put into your case studies twice as effective.

---

1. *Risk sensitivity as an evolutionary adaptation*; Arend Hintze, Randal S. Olson, Christoph
    Adami & Ralph Hertwig, 2015: https://bit.ly/riskFactors
2. I borrow this term from author Nassim Nicholas Taleb who mentions it in his books
    Antifragile and *Skin In the Game*.

CONSIDER THE NEEDS OF YOUR TARGET AUDIENCE

From the hiring manager's perspective, nothing is more of a letdown than a portfolio that has terrible UX. By that I don't mean its look and feel or another such quality that juniors jump to when I give this feedback.

What I mean by terrible UX is when a portfolio lacks consideration for what the person consuming the portfolio expects from it.

UX designers and researchers make the MISTAKE of creating...

- A portfolio **to impress their peers**
- A portfolio of **work that they don't want to do anymore or that is not UX** (e.g. illustration, branding, pure UI work).
- A portfolio of work that has **too many case studies**, none of which are high quality.
- A portfolio that requires the **hiring manager to spend more time than they can allocate** to review a candidate.
- A portfolio that **lacks storytelling** and is often full of screenshots and deliverables only.

All of the above would make your portfolio fail to some extent.

If you can't UX your portfolio, how would you research and design someone else's product or service?

Like with the start of any UX project, when starting your portfolio, you have to think about the user first.

There are two key users of your portfolio: **1) the recruiter, 2) the hiring manager.** These are your two role based archetypes with different user needs, goals, challenges, etc. To better understand what the two expect from candidates and their portfolios, consider the following proto-personas[1]:

THE RECRUITER

About

A middleman between the hiring manager and you

Expertise in UX may vary. Usually is less savvy on UI than UX.

While recruitment is their full-time job, they have a lot of clients and candidates to support

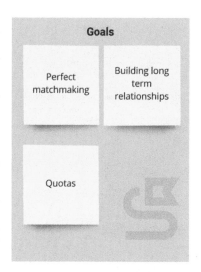

Goals

Perfect matchmaking

Building long term relationships

Quotas

Needs

Easy to follow case studies that are easy to follow and understand

Clearly outlined goals, capability, skills, deliverables, seniority, etc.

Relevant case examples (skills, industry match, channel types, etc.)

Challenges

Mismatch between the candidate's skills on paper and in real life

Unreliable candidates (ghosting, no shows, other offers, etc.)

Limited time to asses the candidates and dig deep into portfolios

Managing expectations for demanding and impatient hiring managers

THE HIRING MANAGER

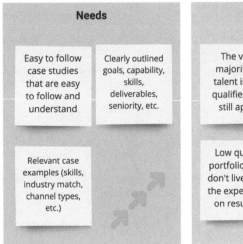

What sticks out the most?

Perhaps that the themes are pretty similar in terms of how you should structure and present your content:

Both will review your resume, portfolio, and case studies and consider all the factors when deciding whether to proceed with your application.

Their goals: While they have other motivations, ultimately, both the recruiter and the hiring manager want to get the right people in at the right time. That is their only goal when reviewing your materials.

Their needs: I left these identical on purpose. While recruiters might have less experience in UX, they are usually told what to look for by the hiring manager. Both proto-personas ultimately need you to:

1. **Tell them that you have the skills, the experience and the evidence to do the job**
2. **Tell a concise story about your approach and dealing with a specific challenge (a case study that guides them)**
3. **Show only the relevant pieces of work, work that you are most proud of and want to do more of**
4. **Support the story with relevant artefacts**
5. **Clearly communicate what you think is proper UX**
6. **Don't BS...**

Their challenges and pain points: Their key challenges are a lack of time pitted against lengthy, unstructured and not UX'd portfolios. Candidates that BS the UX and their experience, as well as candidates who are unqualified, etc.

I hope that the above highlights who you need to think of when working on your UX portfolio and case studies. Make sure to remember that on the receiving end of your portfolio is a human being with their own needs, challenges and goals. Considering these needs will help you write more concise and compelling case studies.

---

1. I didn't want to bloat this book by describing all the different deliverables a designer like you would normally produce in order to deliver better user experiences. However, proto personas are one of those tools that allow teams to quickly outline the key factors about their users. Think of proto personas as the stepping stone towards the more detailed personas, which you're also going to come across in your UX learning.

HOW TO HANDLE CONCEPTUAL
AND NON-COMMERCIAL WORK

Non-commercial, self-directed work might be all that you have when you start practicing UX. That's ok. The worst thing you could do would be to create the impression that conceptual work was real. There's nothing wrong with a conceptual case study, as long as it's good!

As a hiring manager, I'll assess your work like a UX case study regardless of whether it's conceptual or commercial.

What I truly care about is:

1. **Getting a clear sense of your UX knowledge and skills**
2. Seeing how you link the different steps together and **if you know why you do certain activities**
3. Understanding if **specific user research and design skills are up to par** with what's needed in the role
4. Seeing that you understand **the importance of collaboration**, and don't take credit for everything if you worked with others
5. **Understanding the learning and outcomes of your projects.** For example, if your project ended with user testing, make that very clear.

In a conceptual case you can still outline the areas you'd have explored if there weren't limitations (like engaging with developers, iterating, etc.)

but make it clear what was done vs what you'd like to have done with more resources. This isn't just true for conceptual cases; even with commercial projects you can write about where the project would have gone next to showcase your thinking.

The more end-to-end your UX case study is, the better your chances are to get invited for an interview. With every project you work on, make sure to expand the scope and the ways of working.

If you haven't already, in your cases you must cover collaboration with other specialists and stakeholders, different but appropriate methods and activities, lastly also ensure project success by considering both the business and user experience sides.

You might be wondering how the cases are compared and assessed. A simple mental model of how hiring managers view your cases would look like this:

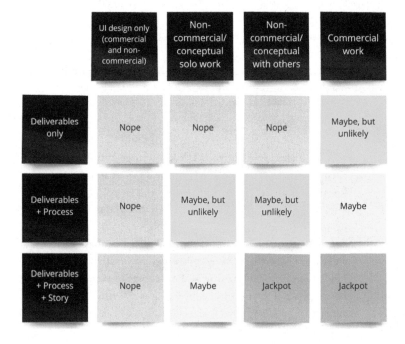

	UI design only (commercial and non-commercial)	Non-commercial/ conceptual solo work	Non-commercial/ conceptual with others	Commercial work
Deliverables only	Nope	Nope	Nope	Maybe, but unlikely
Deliverables + Process	Nope	Maybe, but unlikely	Maybe, but unlikely	Maybe
Deliverables + Process + Story	Nope	Maybe	Jackpot	Jackpot

As you practice your UX skills by applying them to real challenges, the scope of your cases will naturally increase. And as shown in the model above, as this scope progresses so will the status of your portfolio. For now, I recommend clearly labelling your conceptual or non-commercial cases as one of the following: a practice run, an experiment or a way for you to discover and explore new industries, channels, technology or to engage with a new user segment.

∞

TELL A GOOD STORY

Humans are natural storytellers[1]. As we observe the world around us, we formulate stories to fill in the gaps in our understanding. Yet when it's time to tell a story to others, we find it difficult to do so.

The key challenge usually has to do with the ability to retell the story in the engaging enough way, so that the audience understand all the key points as intended. If you followed the advice listed in the previous chapters, then you have by now researched, designed and documented your evidence. The next step is to figure out how to communicate it.

STORYTELLING IN UX CASE STUDIES

I could write a whole book just on storytelling in UX, but the essentials you need to know are few and easy to remember. For example, most of the parts of telling a good story are built on top of a naturally flowing structure – **a story arc** (sometimes referred to as narrative arc):

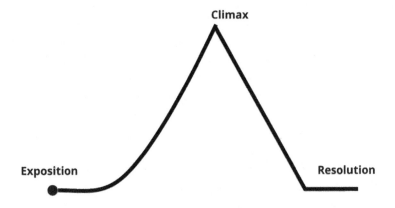

Using this model you can deconstruct every good story into three distinct phases:

- **Exposition and build up to the climax**. This is where you introduce the key players, the landscape, and the environment, and hint at the fundamental challenges. As the story progresses, you uncover more elements. The speed of developments gradually increases.
- **Climax**. The complexity of variables goes through the roof, and our subject is facing a challenge that they need to figure out how to overcome. Finally, the protagonist overcomes the challenge and achieves their goals. Note that if this were a sad story, the outcome would be dismal.
- **Resolution**. This last part covers any knock-on effects of the climax and hints at the future. The resolution is usually short as we already took the audience on a ride in the exposition and the climax.

Now, if we would apply the same story arch principles to a UX case study, it would look something like this:

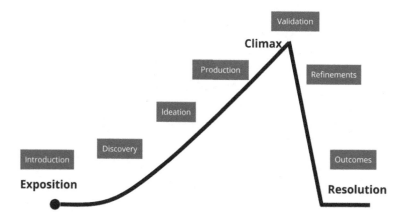

If you'd break this model into smaller bits, each of these phases could be made up of several smaller story arcs. For example, the user research phase alone could have a story or even several stories of its own. You probably have already noticed this in some of the masterfully crafted and engaging books and films: each of those stories is built on the same 3-part set of phases that allow it to resonate with the audience.

At this point you might be worrying about how to come up with those smaller stories or structure them. There's help. Minor storylines can be told using the **SCQA framework** created by author and executive communication consultant Barbara Minto[2] . Many UX designers use this framework to communicate research insights and influence stakeholder decision making.

The SCQA stands for:

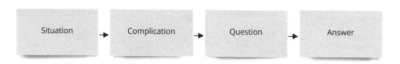

- **Situation**: the stable state of the world. This is something that your audience is aware of.
- **Complication**: The change in that stable state of the world. This is the challenge that your audience is interested in solving.
- **Question**: A question raised by the complication which needs

to be solved. While it can be phrased in different ways, this question should clearly outline a problem.

- **Answer**: The answer to the question raised.

Here's a short (albeit meta) story to better illustrate this structure:

- **Situation:** "As you know, UX design is a challenging, yet very rewarding and impactful career..."
- **Complication:** ".... however, because of its attractiveness, many new UX designers and researchers are facing big competition for a limited number of roles..."
- **Question:** ".... a lot of them also ask me what they can do to stand out from the crowd..."
- **Answer:** "... the answer is simple, but usually not the one they want to hear: improve your storytelling skills to ensure that your work examples showcase your capability to the fullest..."

Can you see how in this example, the SCQA framework can help you tell a better story?

However, a better story isn't necessarily a convincing story as well. To make your story convincing you should add evidence to your Answer. This is explained with another framework, supplementary to the SCQA, Minto's Pyramid Principle:

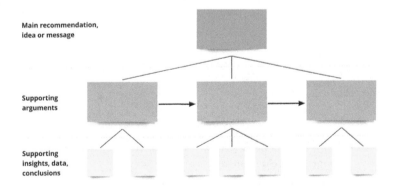

Main recommendation, idea or message

Supporting arguments

Supporting insights, data, conclusions

In this framework, the Answer part of the SCQA becomes the main point. You further enrich that main point using the lower levels of Minto's pyramid.

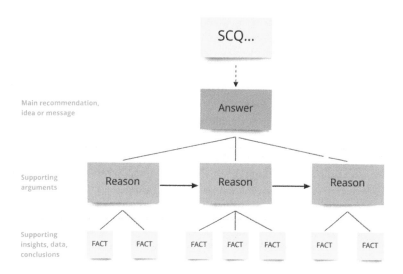

For example, from our Answer ("**the answer is simple, but usually not the one they want to hear: improve your storytelling skills to ensure that your work examples showcase your capability to its fullest...**"), we can form the following supporting arguments:

- **well-crafted stories capture the hiring manager's attention**
- **storytelling reduces cognitive load and conveys the message**
- **storytelling supports the hiring manager's decision-making**

These supporting arguments are further backed up by more specific evidence, factual metrics or insights. For example, the argument that "well-crafted stories capture the hiring manager's attention" **could be supported with evidence from research studies.** A recent exploratory study [3] found that story plot directly impacts the engagement level of the person consuming the content. This finding highlights the importance of interactive storytelling as great stories activate cognitive, emotional, and behavioural responses.

Now, practice on your own example. Try to tell a case study with these three frameworks. Don't stop there. You can also use these frameworks to improve your general communication and ace job interview questions.

FOUR PRACTICAL WAYS TO IMPROVE YOUR STORYTELLING SKILLS

Before you jump into writing your UX case study, you should do some practice. The following four activities are what I do to practice my storytelling skills and come up with killer case study stories.

1. Search, deconstruct and learn from other stories.

The issue with jumping into telling your story (however natural that is) is that you might not yet know what a good story looks like.

That's why as a first step, I'd advise you to seek out good stories, then train your storytelling muscle by deconstructing them:

- **Learn how to plot stories from readily available multimedia**: Netflix, video games, comic books, audio material, news articles, etc., all represent storytelling at its finest. Next time you consume something that entertains you, consider why it is entertaining and try to deconstruct the story with the three frameworks I described in the previous section.
- **Learn UX-focussed storytelling from other designers and their work**: The best way to learn any craft is to steal the methods and ideas from those who are already successful. In the upcoming chapter titled "What good looks like and how to make it even better", I'll list a few portfolios which, some mistakes aside, do tell compelling stories.
- **Learn how to captivate any audience and leave them asking for more**: Verbal articulation is directly linked to human thinking patterns, as established designers already know. So poor storytellers will struggle in any medium because it's their thinking that lacks a flow or structure. They can't deliver key information concisely, with a punch. To see this done well, check out popular public speaking events such as TED Talks which you can watch online. Reflect on how Minto's Pyramid

Principle can be used to share key information in a captivating way.

2. Storyboarding and sketching experiences

So, you have a project, documented assets, and a reason to make it into a case study?

What you should do next is to vomit out as many elements, sound bites and user experience touchpoints as possible. Don't limit yourself at first – you want to get all the ideas out so that you can pick the best ones to communicate your UX project to your portfolio user.

Next, group your ideas or soundbites by affinity (as in the Affinity Mapping activity in UX where you group items by perceived relevance, similarity or purpose). You should end up with several groups of ideas and some overlapping areas.

Now map those groups into a story structure. Use a fixed format such as 2x3 and 3x3 to sketch out the key scenes or slides which in the end might outline:

- **the as-is experience your users faced before the project**
- **the new experience you are developing for users**
- **the ways of working and the process of delivering the new experience**

This should cover all the essential information you need to include in your portfolio case study. It might seem concise but that's the point. You don't want the user to have to skim through your case studies. The way to impress them is to give them just the key information that they want from you.

3. Writing out mini-stories

Imagine that one of your friends asks what you're working on. For whatever reason, you haven't caught up in a while, so they don't know what you've been up to. How would you describe your most recent project to them?

First, you'd think about them as a listener (USER) and then you'd tailor what you say to the context they have.

Now imagine that you have to do this same task, but for whatever reason, you have to answer your friend through an email. Write out what you'd tell them to create a mini-story.

The point of this exercise is to help you outline a short story that would give anyone who reads it a good understanding of your project.

4. Writing out case study drafts

What you can do next is to take the mini-story from the previous exercise and add context to it to make it a fully-fledged case study. After adding context to your points, build on it even further by attaching the right illustrative assets (photos, diagrams, maps, deliverable shots).

If you do all of this, you will end up with a solid case study. While building out your draft, consider the following advice:

- **Add more detail than you need, then delete at least half of it.** Prune your case study until you can't remove any more information. Less is more, just like with all things designed.
- **Apply formatting to help your target audience see the key information**: use headlines and quotes, and bold what should stand out.
- **Show, don't tell.** However, only add imagery to support the story points that need illustrating.
- **Ask for help and honest advice from people who are slightly more senior** than you in their careers. Ask them to highlight any points in your case study that are confusing or need more insights. Ask them what stands out to them as the most effective.

Stories are all around you. You must repeatedly attempt to observe, deconstruct and learn from them. Over time, this practice of reading into good stories and crafting your own will make you a better communicator.

∞

1. *Storytelling as Adaptive Collective Sensemaking*, Lucas M. Bietti, Ottilie Tilston, Adrian Bangerter, 2017. Topics in Cognitive Science published by Wiley Periodicals, Inc. on behalf of Cognitive Science Society.
2. The recommended further reading, courses and other learning material from Barbara Minto: https://bit.ly/barbaraMinto
3. How stories generate consumer engagement: An exploratory study. Journal of Business Research

PICK THE RIGHT PORTFOLIO PLATFORM

Many designers get bogged down with picking the right platform for their UX portfolios. In reality, it doesn't matter where you put your work; what really matters is what you do with it.

If I had to pick the perfect platform for UX portfolios, it would have the following capabilities:

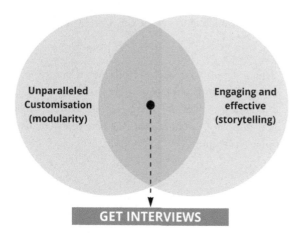

Customisable

- Highly customisable layout; fully controllable in terms of content
- Modular: the ability to handle multiple case studies; tailor the selection of case studies for each new job application as necessary

Engaging

- Good overall UX for you and your portfolio users: simple, usable, accessible
- Help tell a story the way you want it to be read and perceived

There are, of course, a tonne of websites that can showcase the evidence of your craft. However, because I'm often asked which platform I'd recommend, I'd presume that people can't find an option that ticks all the boxes.

Most platforms out there aren't great for getting you a UX job. You already know from a previous chapter that **it's easy to build a portfolio to impress your peer designers but it's harder to build a portfolio for landing a UX research or design role.**

That's why you should separate your branding activities and the work made to impress peer designers from the work you submit to get job interviews.

Of course, depending on your work's depth and relevance, you can have an online presence to both impress and get hired but most people will need to be careful how they market themselves in different situations. This is the crucial reason why I draw a clear line between these use cases and the platform that fits them.

PLATFORMS THAT ARE GREAT FOR NETWORKING PURPOSES (AND IMPRESSING YOUR PEERS)

Many case studies on these platforms are shallow (often just conceptual UI-focussed studies) with little to no UX (no user research focus).

With some exceptions, unless hiring managers are looking for UI or product designers, they rarely go to these places to look for potential talent: *Dribbble, Behance, Coroflot,* and similar.

If your goal is to collect feedback on UI or creative work and be a part of a much larger peer community, then these platforms do serve your purpose. As a UX hiring manager and someone who has seen countless portfolios across these sites, I don't recommend using them for your UX portfolio.

PLATFORMS THAT ARE GREAT FOR DEMONSTRATING THE EVIDENCE AND GETTING INTO UX

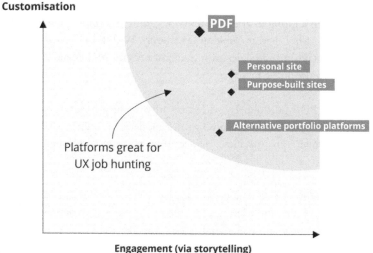

Now that we got that 'other' portfolio category out the way, it's time to dig into the real deal. The following list of platforms is what you should consider as the basis for your most effective UX portfolio.

The best choice, all things considered: the PDF portfolio

Wait, a PDF?

Yes. I've yet to find a better option, that covers all those key factors that a portfolio platform should have. The blank pages of a PDF are a freeform canvas to which you can add stories, imagery, and whatever else your heart desires.

Furthermore, because almost any tool (Acrobat, Pages, Word, Miro, Figma, Sketch, etc.) these days allows you to export to PDF, the opportunities to showcase your work in the right way are infinite.

The best part about a PDF portfolio is that you can make it modular.

For example, you could have a case study for every project you worked on in the past. This could naturally end up being a hefty portfolio that is impossible to attach to a job application.

But to grab a hiring manager's attention, you need to make your portfolio relevant to what they are looking for anyway. With a PDF portfolio, you can easily take out the slides with the most relevant studies and share only those with the hiring manager.

My own PDF portfolio is a selection of over fifty quality case studies covering deep UX research, product design, decision support, AI, innovation, mobile app specifics, service design, team development, and design ops.

If I'd apply for a role that needs user research, service design and design ops, I would pick the relevant case studies for those areas and assemble a brand new portfolio for my application. Just like a resume or cover letter should be edited for each individual job, so should your portfolio.

Having a modular portfolio allows you tailor and assemble new set of evidence quickly:

Your modular case study bank collected over time:

Research focus

↑

Service design	Behavioural design	Store experience
Recruitment experience	eCommerce website	Digital service
Omni-channel experience	Employee platform	Decision support
Data viz	Website	VR experience
Mobile app	Design system	Design system

UX

↓

UI focus

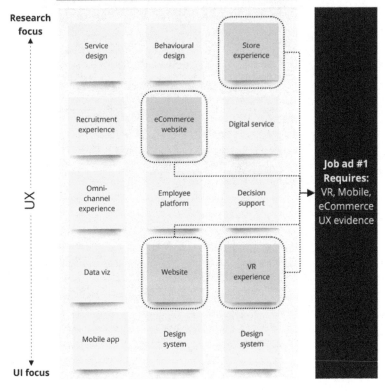

2 **Tailoring to specific job applications - pick only relevant case studies:**

Research focus

UX

UI focus

Service design

Behavioural design

Store experience

Recruitment experience

eCommerce website

Digital service

Omni-channel experience

Employee platform

Decision support

Data viz

Website

VR experience

Mobile app

Design system

Design system

Job ad #1 Requires: VR, Mobile, eCommerce UX evidence

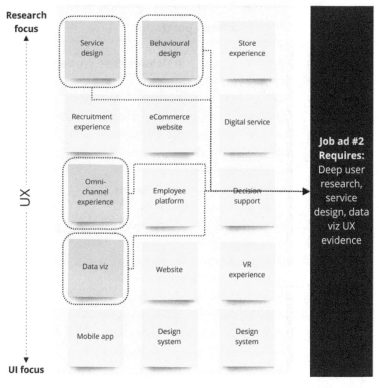

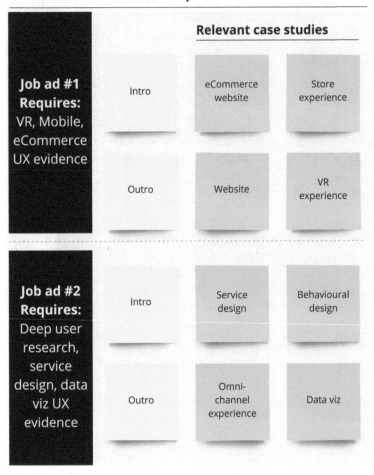

3 Make new portfolios in PDF and apply for the job:

Tailored portfolios

Relevant case studies

| Job ad #1 Requires: VR, Mobile, eCommerce UX evidence | Intro | eCommerce website | Store experience |
| | Outro | Website | VR experience |

| Job ad #2 Requires: Deep user research, service design, data viz UX evidence | Intro | Service design | Behavioural design |
| | Outro | Omni-channel experience | Data viz |

As someone who wants to get into UX, you might only have one, two or three case studies but even then, you should aim to set up a working PDF portfolio that can scale as you add more to it.

It's worth noting that the best candidates I've had the pleasure of interviewing and hiring all had their work in PDFs. Because of its flexibility, ease of use, customisation and relative control of privacy, it's a go-to choice for many experienced designers who are there to get the top jobs.

$$\infty$$

NOT THE BEST BUT STILL GOOD: A PERSONAL WEBSITE YOU HAVE COMPLETE CONTROL OVER

While anyone can benefit from having a future-proof domain (e.g., "*yourname.com*"), personal website or a blog, this is a secondary choice for a reason. Having a unique site means financial investment and learning skills that aren't benefiting you as a UX designer.

Another thing to consider is how you control the privacy of your work. That said, at the start of your career privacy might not matter as most of your work are likely side projects, concept cases, bootcamp case studies, and the like.

Personal websites you can customise and own provide you with a little less customisation than a PDF but they can be a good alternative. A personal website also allows you to start a blog.

A good option that will not require any advanced[1] technical skills to get started is Wordpress.org (note this is not the .com version of Wordpress). You'd want to get a Wordpress theme that is crafted for portfolio content.

For example, *Semplice* is a good add-on portfolio maker environment that plugs into the standard WordPress package. Just make sure to keep the usability and accessibility in check. Some of the options they offer do not follow best UX principles and could take away from your portfolio's effectiveness.

$$\infty$$

STILL ACCEPTABLE: PURPOSE-BUILT PORTFOLIO SITES AND WEBSITE GENERATORS

I'm not a fan of these unless you have complete technical control of the hosting, the domain, CMS, underlying codebase and other factors that allow for pivotal enhancements or big structural tweaks. While these might not matter to you at first, they will become more relevant as you grow. If you'd ask me to choose between a website I can fully control or one that comes out of the box, I'd pick the former.

While purpose-built website makers can help get you set up quickly, they also tend to be limiting in terms of storytelling abilities.

I've yet to see a purpose-built UX portfolio site that does justice to UX, not just UI. Most portfolio sites support visual presentation over substance, research, and steps to arrive at the solution.

For those who might still be interested in ready-made solutions, here's some to look into:

- *Wix*
- *Squarespace*
- *Wordpress.com (not to be confused with .org)*
- *Adobe Portfolio*
- *Carbonmade*
- *Cargo*

ALTERNATIVE PORTFOLIO PLATFORMS

If none of the portfolio options discussed so far work for you, then here's some more alternatives that might surprise you:

- **An Axure prototype**. I was recently sent a link to an Axure prototype that worked like any other portfolio. The sheer possibilities of using such a medium impressed me because Axure technically has an unlimited freeform canvas. It renders as a website, you can export it, upload it to the cloud, host it under your own domain, use variables and other innovative high fidelity features without code. Finally, you can also password protect your proto-portfolio.
- **A Youtube channel**. You can host video case studies and other engaging material. It's much easier to tell a story with

multimedia. However, you will need some skills to be able to produce presentable material. Also, this is relevant mainly for work examples that you can show off publicly.

- **LinkedIn**. The often overlooked features on Linkedin profiles include the ability to add full-fledged UX case studies, attach PDFs, links to products that went live, videos of prototypes, pictures of the process. All as featured material on your profile page! For example, if you've worked at Acme Ltd., you can add a file URL or attachment to that work history entry to better illustrate some of the outcomes. In effect, you are enriching a typical Linkedin resume with UX portfolio elements.

- **Notion**. How can a note-taking app be a good option for UX designers or researchers? Because it provides the ability to publish pretty unique websites out of your notes. I recently reviewed four different portfolios that were done in Notion. It seems it's becoming a go-to, low-code tool.

Now that you know the platforms I recommend, I will share some example UX portfolios that take different approaches.

---

1. HTML, CSS, and basic Javascript-based websites require prior knowledge of essential web technologies and front-end engineering. While most of this can be learned in a matter of days, depending on how much time you can spend on crafting your portfolio, I'd prioritise actual UX work or polishing case studies so they tell a better story..

WHAT GOOD LOOKS LIKE AND
HOW TO MAKE IT EVEN BETTER

To put everything we've learned so far together, the best UX portfolios are usually made from the following parts:

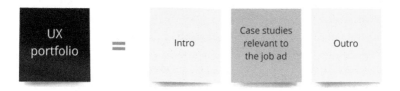

- **The intro.** This would be a snappy intro to you as a person, your key skills, key career highlights and aspirations, approach to UX design, your personal design principles, and anything else that introduces you as a UX practitioner. The more you develop your UX skills, the richer this section will become.
- **Case studies relevant to the job ad.** This should be a few pieces of work that you think would best resonate with the hiring manager or recruiter. For a junior, 1-3 case studies should be enough. Instead of focussing on numbers, focus on QUALITY. After all, UX is a synonym for quality as we already established.
- **The outro:** other information that might be relevant to the role you're applying for. For example, if you have a blog, Twitter profile, LinkedIn page or anything else that is publicly

accessible and potentially relevant - add a link. Another great way to finish off the portfolio is to add a hook that encourages the hiring managers to reach out to you, along the lines of "Get in touch to find out more".

EXAMPLES OF REAL UX PORTFOLIOS

On my YouTube channel *vaexperience*, I review portfolios submitted by viewers from UX, product design and user research.

In each review I share specific advice on how their portfolios could be improved. **Most often this advice is about storytelling, about artefacts used to support said story, or about the lack of deep user research.**

Coming up, you'll find a selection of those video reviews. To make it easier for you, the selected videos are each 10-15 minutes long. I'd recommend you to watch as many of these as possible and start noting down the take-aways. Try to find the underlying advice that is repeated to build your own checklist that you can use now as well as in the future when you need to audit your portfolio again.

Junior design portfolios:

- A portfolio with a case study that needs storytelling improvements and restructuring: https://bit.ly/UXPortfolioReview1
- A junior's first portfolio with a case study that mixes up design thinking and UX: https://bit.ly/UXPortfolioReview2
- A portfolio where the case study is split into separate pages for design and research: https://bit.ly/UXPortfolioReview3
- An over-designed portfolio, or why creativity can backfire: https://bit.ly/UXPortfolioReview4
- A junior designer who wanted to introduce a brand new app, and the challenges of trying to make products in our service-driven world: https://bit.ly/UXPortfolioReview5

Mid, senior and beyond portfolios:

- Content-rich portfolio of a product designer that would

double its effectiveness with a bit more research: https://bit.ly/UXPortfolioReview6

- The portfolio of an enterprise-level designer that needs just a bit more user research: https://bit.ly/UXPortfolioReview7
- The portfolio of a freelance designer who wants to join an in-house design team: https://bit.ly/UXPortfolioReview8
- A designer who uses a lot of text to tell a story, but very few visual artefacts: https://bit.ly/UXPortfolioReview9
- A designer who hints at work under NDA without breaking any legal agreements: https://bit.ly/UXPortfolioReview10

You can view many more reviews in this playlist: https://bit.ly/UXPortfolioReviews

EVIDENCE VS POTENTIAL

When reviewing candidate portfolios, the two factors that any hiring manager will look for are the documented evidence and the potential to do the work. While I've already gone into depth about the importance of proving your skills and work capability with evidence, I only hinted at the idea of potential. Unlike evidence, which you can collect through hard work, potential is harder to influence, though not impossible:

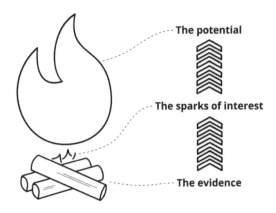

The potential

The sparks of interest

The evidence

Your potential is a particularly critical part to consider when starting in UX or any other field. The current state of the UX job market is dire. Hiring managers are struggling to find talent among all the pseudo-UX work. They are looking for work examples that are complex enough, deeply researched and relevant to their problems. If it meets the criteria, your evidence will get them interested but it's your potential that will get them to invite you for an interview.

To influence and boost the potential hiring managers see in you, you should have the following:

- A UX portfolio that shows a **good understanding of the UX process**, especially the depth of user research
- **Relevant experience** in the industry assessed by project type, channels, technology, challenge, users, and many other factors. The more relevant experience you have, the more potential you have to hit the ground running.
- **An eye for quality**. While the visual presentation of your portfolio matters a lot, it's not as important as the quality of the underlying UX process. You should do UX research by the book without skipping or faking it, pick the right methods, then go above and beyond to tell an engaging story that covers all the key steps you took. This will take time to develop but it's needed for a killer portfolio.
- **Evident passion for design**, research, or any other field which requires you to solve problems by putting users first. For

example, someone who comes from psychology, social sciences, design or architecture, or someone who has worked with other people, could have enough potential to take on UX even if their experience is shallow.

- **Evidence, in the form of case studies**, that the candidate is capable of doing the fundamental experience design activities without sacrificing the QUALITY of said methods.
- **Peripheral materials** that are well built, especially the cover letter through which you express a passion for UX.
- Visibly **going above and beyond** to ensure that you target the correct problems, challenge business assumptions and champion real user needs. If you make any compromises, you don't sweep them under the rug. Instead, you take full ownership and explain why.
- **Social presence** and design community participation. For example, many designers these days also blog or engage in other efforts to attach to their portfolio as thoughts, interests, etc. While this one is not necessary, it can add cheap points to your potential. For example, I've been blogging, making videos, and writing newsletters on UX for a few years, and some people who interviewed me as a candidate highlighted those activities as a positive.
- **Interpersonal skills** and everything to do with collaboration, trust-building, stakeholder management and other related softer skills. Some of the best juniors I've hired included photos of them working with other people in their portfolios. This is another cheap shot, but it tells a story of you working with others and collaborating. If you don't have photos to display (don't use stock photos!), you could highlight how you work with others in writing. You could be the most talented UX designer in the world, but if you can't communicate and work well with others, you won't be a desirable candidate.

If you think that your portfolio case studies are spot on but you still can't get in, it could be that something is missing in your evidence. The hiring manager doesn't see enough potential in you yet. If you can invest some extra time to improve these areas, you're still more likely to stand out from the crowd of applicants who do the bare minimum.

∞

PREPARE THE PERIPHERAL ASSETS

While your portfolio is the primary tool to break into the UX field, there are also a few peripheral assets that you should tidy up before you start applying for jobs.

After putting a lot of effort into their portfolios, many designers rush through updating their resumes and LinkedIn profiles, or they don't update them at all. This shocks me because these assets also contribute to your potential and evidence.

Recently, I reviewed several UX candidates for an open role and a couple of them forgot to submit their resumes. This is not unusual. UX designers tend to combine their resumes with portfolios in one pack, which is neither good nor bad, as long as the hiring manager can find both without struggle. In these two cases though, the candidates only submitted their portfolio links and nothing else.

As a hiring manager, I don't have time to hunt for clues but I often have to do it anyway because asking the recruiter to follow up with the candidate would take too long. Both portfolios included links to LinkedIn, so in the absence of their resumes, I looked at their LinkedIn pages to understand their experience.

Both profiles were almost empty. Imagine a few entries of work history including only the job title and company name, with no supporting information. Since their portfolios weren't outstanding compared to other applicants, I passed on these two candidates.

Always do a bit more than is enough. Before applying, fill out your LinkedIn profile with supportive information, add a link to your portfolio, attach your resume and, if appropriate, a cover letter. Consider your users who have absolutely no time to do additional detective work. As with everything UX - the easier you can make it for your audience, the better the overall experience will be.

At a minimum you should consider investing time and updating the following assets:

A PRESENTABLE AND TRUTHFUL LINKEDIN PROFILE

What you need to do make your LinkedIn profile presentable is the following:

- **A simple photo** of you looking professional.
- **Switch on the "Open to work" flag** on your profile. This option shows your profile to recruiters who are looking for UX designers through the LinkedIn search. The flag is also a cue for any hiring managers who might come across your profile in other ways, such as from the feed.
- **The title**: this appears directly under your name. Ideally, it should say "Junior UX designer. Open to new opportunities," or something similar. Highlight your current skill level and what you're looking for.
- **The links**: you can and should embed anything you've produced so far. For example, case study links, YouTube vids,

blog articles, project websites, etc. Reflect what's most appropriate to insert and add a couple of links that can make things easier for any people who stumble upon your profile.

- **The summary**: keep it short and expand on your experience and interest in the UX field. Remember, this is where you can add all the keywords to increase your chances of being found, but use them meaningfully. The summary should explain your current skill set and what you're looking for next.

- **Work experience and education**: what matters most is your UX-related design experience. However, you must also add any other knowledge (as described before, any degree is relevant in its way). While education is easy to add, work experience might be trickier. That's why I always recommend adding all internships, shadowing opportunities, freelancing work blocks, etc.

- **Courses and certificates**: don't just add the courses you've taken, include a few lines about what you learned from them. Doing so could also add keywords to make your profile more discoverable on LinkedIn search.

- **Skill endorsements:** ask people who you know (from past work or studies) to endorse your UX-specific skills. If you haven't yet worked with anyone - share examples of the work you've done and ask them to give you endorsements based on those examples.

- **Social recommendations**: use ALL your friends, peers and junior UX designers to social proof your profile. You can request their recommendations immediately to be displayed on your profile for the public to see. This is often an overlooked feature but is essential to provide social proof and personalise your profile. Different recommendations will also probably highlight different aspects of what makes you a good designer so they'll create a more holistic view of your core competencies.

- **Who you follow and your groups**: one of the last parts of any profile is the interests' shelf which contains all the people (thought leaders), companies and groups you're following or are a member of. Use the LinkedIn search first to find the ones most relevant to your craft and UX in general. Be genuine in picking what you're interested in. It will show the more aspirational side of you.

All of the above items act as signals picked up by the LinkedIn search engine. Don't use popular keywords just for the sake of it but if you keep things truthful, they might just help you be discovered by a recruiter. This is a passive way to be found but it doesn't harm to have it in place in addition to your other applications. A well-presented LinkedIn profile will be impressive when a hiring manager does see it as a peripheral asset.

As a junior who wants to break into UX, you have to put effort into your peripherals, especially your public, professional profiles like LinkedIn. Simply updating your profile with some relevant information can boost engagement and get you more outreach from recruiters.

A TAILORED RESUME

Like with the LinkedIn profile, you need to tailor your resume to reflect your skills and experience as right for the role. The mistake most UX designers make is over-designing the look of their resumes instead of focussing on its content. The look and feel will not get your foot in the door.

Regardless of how much experience you have, your resume should remain a simple, primarily text-based document. Remember that you're not applying for the job of a graphic designer; poor resume design can hurt you more than good design can help.

Here's a challenge I always give to juniors who want their resumes reviewed: stick to plain text, no imagery, photos, or colours. Only add formatting to important content such as headlines. There are a couple of big reasons for this:

1. **A UX hiring manager will spend less time on your resume than your portfolio, so the content needs to be scannable.**
2. **Some companies will have automated applicant management systems (ATS) that confuse and mix**

everything up when applicants make their resumes into an art project. Your resume will get thrown out before it's even been seen.

I've witnessed UX designers and researchers who submitted the automated export of their LinkedIn profile as their resume (a basic PDF) and they outperformed candidates who had over-designed resumes.

As with portfolios, a critical thing to consider is the usability of your resume and how its user (the recruiter, the hiring manager) will consume it. That's why the critical takeaway here is that you should spend whatever time you have working on your portfolio, as it matters more.

The things hiring managers want to see in resumes:

- **Experience:** List years in the field, commercial experience or anything close to it to assess your capability. Never state obvious or redundant information. Some designers go overboard explaining each UX activity they did. This is even worse when their every job experience has the same list of activities. Make sure to list the unique value-add, which brings me to my next point...
- **Achievements:** What have you done that's benefited the business or the end-users? Focus on your results rather than your job duties to make your resume more compelling. Did you improve conversion rates? Or help users achieve their goals more efficiently? Be specific about the improvements, or even better, quantify them. Even if you might think a project didn't achieve anything, think again. You can find achievements even for conceptual projects or projects that failed. Dig deep and find the themes that will show how your involvement contributed to valuable outcomes.
- **Projects**: By now, you should be religiously working on your side projects. List any relevant side projects, conceptual cases, and other work that doesn't fit under Experience to amplify your resume's impact. The more relevant your resume is to the industry, target users, and challenges of the potential employer, the more likely you are to be picked out of the applicant pool.
- **Skills**: Even without a track record or commercial experience,

you'll have learned many techniques and skills. Some will be highly technical, others more strategic or interpersonal. List them out, and don't forget to add how proficient you are in them. Many juniors these days add a slider or progress bars to showcase their experience but that's too vague. A simple "Interaction design: advanced" will be received much better than a cute progress bar that could mean anything.

- **Education:** This is least important for experienced UX designers, but it matters more for those new to the field. I'd recommend listing all relevant degrees, courses, certificates, diplomas, anything that supports your journey into UX, etc. This section helps but not having it won't ruin your chances alone.

Depending on the seniority of the role you're applying for, the order of importance of the above items will vary. **Generally your track record and achievements are the most important parts.**

I recently published a crash course video on making UX resumes. Check it out at the following link as it goes into more depth on everything I've mentioned so far: https://bit.ly/UXresumes101.

Note that some regions and countries have different cultural standards. After publishing that video, I learned that my viewers' resumes in Switzerland, Japan, and other countries have specific (even if unwritten) requirements.

For example, whilst I would discourage candidates from adding their photos on their resumes in the UK, in other regions it's a requirements that might prevent you from progressing in the interview process.

As with any other bit in this book, you may have to adjust my advice to apply it to the culture where you are job-hunting. This is also part of knowing your user and adapting your resume or portfolio to different scenarios.

∞

A TAILORED COVER LETTER

I always hated writing cover letters and thought they were passé. However, for juniors who don't have a rich resume or portfolio, a good cover letter can be a game-changer. Most other people won't invest the time so, if you do, you could stand out.

Here's why cover letters are great:

- **You can tell a story about yourself without being constrained by the formats** of other mediums such as the resume or your social profiles.
- **You can tailor your application even further and add anecdotal evidence** that doesn't fit in your resume. Remember, resumes will be reviewed by the USER – recruiters and hiring managers. Recruiters want it to display standard information while hiring managers will look for relevance in the evidence.
- If you don't have much to show in your UX portfolio yet, you want to double down in your cover letter to **explain who you are and why you're passionate about UX**. Share your aspirations and anything else that can help sell you as the right designer for the person reviewing your application.

In all, if you can produce a tailored half-pager for each application, you'll be more likely to stand out and connect with hiring managers as a person.

A few tips on how to write an effective cover letter:

- **Keep it concise and straightforward:** 2-3 paragraphs, a few hundred words tops should do the trick. Think of your cover letter as a small to mid-sized email that can be read within a minute or two.
- **Introduce yourself:** your background, learning journey, relevant interests and goals going forward. Make it very clear what your long-term career goals are and why your engagement is critical for the potential employer.
- **Highlight where your interests overlap:** share why this is a great opportunity for you, but more importantly, also share

what you bring to the table. List out some of the areas you could contribute from a UX perspective, mention skills, previous project work, relevant links and more.

- **Add a hook:** direct their attention to your resume and portfolio. Use the cover letter as a guiding tool to get more permission and attention from the users. Make sure that the resume does the same and flows into the portfolio.

Think of the cover letter as your elevator pitch. What makes elevator pitches successful is not listing just dry facts that can be found on your resume, but communicating the value you offer and creating a human connection. As before, consider the actual needs and realities of your target audience - what would they need to hear to make a positive decision?

∞

FAQS

Do I need to tailor my resume, cover letter and portfolio for every application?

Yes. Especially when you're getting started. Even the experienced folk will be more likely to land an interview if they showcase the evidence that is relevant to the position that they're after. This is precisely why tailoring your content is a habit you should start fostering immediately. No exceptions.

You said you would spend only a few minutes reviewing the applications. So why bother with the peripherals?

It takes a few minutes to make a well-informed assessment in terms of relevancy, UX research and design skills, etc. It doesn't mean you should ignore the rest. Quite the opposite, if your UX case studies spark interest, you can rest assured that the rest of your material will be looked at as well.

Think of all this material as tools to cover the gaps and invite the potential hiring manager for the interview – you need to quite literally get them hooked on the story of you.

∞

CHAPTER 6

GET THE JOB

"The truth is simple: If you want to be a leader, then lead. If you want to be a writer, then write. 'I am of service' is something each of us can choose to become. It only takes a moment to begin."

SETH GODIN

It's time to share everything you learned and produced from previous chapters with your target audience. Think of this step as a pseudo user testing effort where your information design and prototypes will either stick with the user or they will need further improvements.

To stick it and land the job, there are just three things you still need to consider at this point: you should only apply for the right roles to match your needs with particular employer needs, secondly, you'll need to overcome internal and external resistance, and lastly you'll need to pass the interview stage which can be challenging.

In this chapter, I'll break down how you can approach and address each of these three things. Don't overlook this information because these last few steps can make a big difference to the success of your application.

THE NEW SET OF BLOCKERS YOU MUST OVERCOME

In the 'Consider your starting point' chapter describing internal blockers, my bold take was that the majority of challenges any new designer faces on their journey to getting a UX job will be a combination of internalised blockers and external challenges and dependencies.

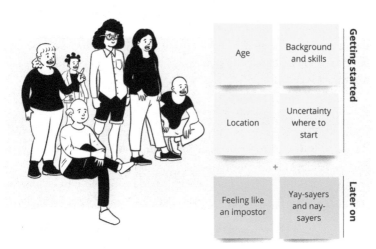

I'm sure you've already experienced self-doubt, impostor syndrome, and uncertainty regarding what steps to take next. Maybe even snarky commentary. Recalling my first couple of years of trying to get into UX, I listened to every input and in the end was left confused - I didn't know where to start or if my skills were market-ready.

In the following sections, I will cover how to deal with these blockers so that, even if you can't overcome them, you can still move forward.

FEELING LIKE AN IMPOSTOR

If you feel like an impostor, it's probably because you are one. That's not a bad thing!

We all fear rejections, feeling inadequate or being called out for the things we do. Deep down, we want to be competent. We want to fit in and contribute value to the immediate community and the broader society. But because we can't tell if we are capable enough, we feel like impostors.

Impostor syndrome is a natural occurrence that comes with growth. It's something you feel when you're challenging yourself, when you're over-reaching to learn and apply new things, doing things for the first time or in a different context.

Impostor syndrome is also very prevalent in our community and it's one of the questions I get asked the most (from both juniors and seniors): how do I overcome feeling like an impostor? I always recommend that you face reality and accept this feeling as part of your growth.

But here's the trick: while everyone faces the same self-doubt and fear some people still persevere and learn from it. **Know that everyone feels the same way, and everyone's an impostor. Until they are not**. Every-one, myself included, is just trying to figure things out. While some things are easy to make up, others take experimentation. You need to be brave to choose yourself, and to do things that might not come to you naturally.

The Dunning-Kruger model illustrates this point perfectly: with each new commitment to acquire proficiency you'll face a lengthy period of feeling like an impostor. In fact, I'd vouch that feeling like an impostor usually lasts the longest or perhaps we just notice it the most compared to any other phase of our development:

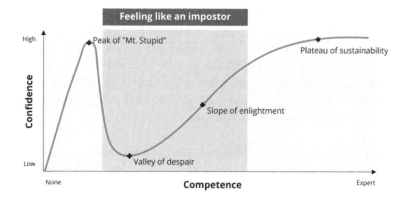

If you plot this effect over the rest of your career, you can see that you will feel like an impostor again and again whenever you try to progress:

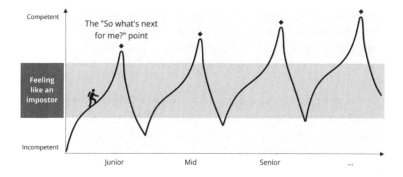

You can also see that the key to overcoming impostor syndrome and bringing that curve up is to become more competent at the things you repeatedly do. The more you do something, the better you get at it. So you become more confident. You realise you are indeed capable so you feel less like an impostor. The syndrome will fade with repetition and continuous validation that you are indeed on the right path. Every repetition of methods helps you chip away at that self-doubt and fear.

As someone who wants to get into UX, you are supposed to feel like an impostor because you are one. In Seth Godin's words, "*Time spent fretting about our status as impostors is time away from dancing with our fear, from leading and from doing work that matters.*"

BE CAREFUL WHO YOU FOLLOW

Because of the high market fragmentation and general confusion about what UX is and what it is not, there are a lot of individuals whose efforts to evangelise will directly impact how you feel about yourself. Some will make you feel like you're overthinking UX, others will put you down because you are not doing UX hard enough.

As a UX designer I like to think in archetypes that describe people based on their behaviours (you are what you do). Over time I've observed two distinct archetypes on social and analog channels and you will come across both of these in your journey: the yay-sayers and the nay-sayers.

The yay-sayers

The yay-sayers are the people who benefit from making things seem simpler than they need to be. These are typically inexperienced design evangelists (often presenting as influencers) who focus on the glossy UI work and mislabel it as UX. More often than not, they label everything UX and sometimes even have opposing views.

Just the other day, I encountered a Lead UX/UI designer advising people to design more and research less. I'm not sure what made them a leader to begin with, but they are not someone you should listen to. Especially if you care for your career in actual UX.

This archetype also includes the gurus who promise quick results and guaranteed job opportunities. In reality, they rarely deliver as the state of the market is that there are too many entry-level designers, meanwhile, the hiring managers can't find enough UX designers who can do the job well.

The yay-sayers might provide a continuous motivation drip that helps you get inspired, but that's about it. There's usually very little substance to their content or actionable advice.

The naysayers

If the yay-sayers are the happy spokesmen, the nay-sayers are the opposite: dogmatists, frequently old-timers seeping with frustration and bitterness at the current state of the UX job market. Sometimes their pessimism is justified, but often not at all. Every social media network has at least a few people who are very quick to criticise others and try to be correct regardless of the context (which often is completely ignored or not sought after).

These are people who are quick to use their credentials to support highly opinionated claims and generally seem to thrive from putting other people down. This approach tends to fall short and alienate not just the up-and-coming designers, but also the ones who want to change the industry for the better.

So who should you follow?
User experience is a vast field with many possible methods and activities, some more appropriate than others. At this stage in your journey, you should find and follow people who can guide you through the field without forcing their dogmas on you or belittling your attempts to learn.

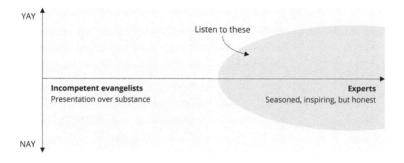

As you read the above, I hope you can already identify some of these dogmatists and evangelists in your circles. Sadly, they tend to be the loudest folk in the UX design and research industry while the silent majority are more pragmatic, positive, supportive and invested in helping designers like yourself grow.

And let me be clear - I'm not separating myself from either. I produce both types of content and have very strong opinions when it comes to design standards, pragmatism and what UX should be about. However, I truly try to base my approach on human-centric methods - making sure that my goals consider the people who are on the receiving end.

The key takeaway here is to steer clear from the extremes in opinions and experience. Instead, focus on people who can lift you up and help you move forward. What's even more important is that they also give you critical feedback without putting you down.

The best people to learn from are the ones that can do both: yay-saying and nay-saying as appropriate to the context. You don't want sugar-coating, but you shouldn't want just negativity either.

∞

WHERE TO APPLY AND WHAT TO LOOK FOR

Job openings are easy to find but not all openings are equal or suitable for UX designers, as compared to hybrid roles, UI focused positions and other opportunities.

There are several factors that I recommend all juniors consider when picking their first opportunities:

- **Opportunities where you can shadow and learn from a senior colleague**
- **Prospects that have a clear need for proper UX**
- **Options that provide an excellent experimentation ground for your newly discovered skills**
- **All of the above**

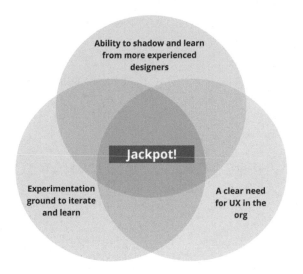

For example, money and reward should not be the key factor you look for in your first role. Of course you should be able to cover your expenses and be paid reasonably for the local market. However, instead of going after more money I'd advise you to prioritise learning. The money should follow as your skills improve and you deliver value on each and every project.

Understandably, you can't be too picky at the beginning of your career; however, having clearly defined criteria (just like in user research) will guide you in the right direction. Even if some job ads share the same title you must asses each and every opportunity individually. You should use the bulleted list or venn diagram above to ask yourself if a specific job description ticks each factor off.

FIND PLACEMENTS IN STARTUPS

Startups are probably the best places to gain hands-on experience in the shortest amount of time, as you'll be thrown into action immediately. Because you'll need to wear multiple hats, all your technical, interpersonal and strategic skills will be tested to the limit. While some startups will have an established visual language, product design or UX process, others are more likely to rely on you to help them develop it. Regardless, you'll be able to drive user-centricity and have an impact, thanks to the flexible and nimble ways of working.

Just make sure you don't sacrifice the QUALITY of UX for a faster delivery. The worst thing you could do would be to join a startup and start churning out UI design work calling it UX, without learning or developing the way you want to. Your portfolio will gather dust and when it's time to find the next opportunity, you'll be left with little evidence to get it.

It's worth noting that startup work-life is not for everyone and some new designers could struggle in such an environment. If that's what you're worried about, make sure that the team has someone who can show you the ropes, or they can give you enough time and freedom to practice.

All things considered, if you think startups are right for you, you can look for placements on Angel list, Product hunt, LinkedIn or in local startup communities. Even outside of those places, job ads now commonly state when a role is in a startup environment.

If I were you, I'd email at least a handful of them with my evidence and my peripherals.

∞

FIND INTERNSHIPS OR APPRENTICESHIPS IN ESTABLISHED STUDIOS AND AGENCIES

Note, that depending on where you're located internships and apprenticeships could be paid or unpaid. As you'd expect, paid opportunities are also the ones that have the most competition.

If you have more experience and a great starter UX portfolio, you could apply for apprenticeships at established companies or more mature and larger startups. An official apprenticeship provides a different environment from a startup.

There will be a set of expectations and standards that junior designers will have to meet. Likely, they'll also have a designer who will assess your work, and whilst you can never tell who's on the receiving end, if you apply for companies that are doing well, you need a strong portfolio.

I've worked with apprentices who had strong portfolios for their experience level but they couldn't contribute much to actual client work because of the company culture. Instead, they'd be asked to make coffee or do admin work that no one else wanted to do. That's not the sort of apprenticeship you want.

If you end up in such situation, there are things you can do in order to be trusted with actual work. You need to have the right attitude. Being proactive, taking ownership of tasks and assisting people around you will go a long way. Make sure to show initiative so that people invariably learn to trust you and the UX skills you bring to the table.

While startup opportunities for entry-level designers are aplenty, internships and apprenticeships are rare. You should reach out directly to the most senior UX and design person in the organisation, agency or studio to get ahead. They usually have good insight as to what gaps there are in their team. Again: research, shortlist, mass email. But most importantly, make sure that your portfolio and peripheral tools are glowing.

REACH OUT TO THE PEOPLE IN YOUR NETWORK

A professional network takes a long time to develop. However, even the connections you've made so far, however small they might seem, could help you find a job. It takes very little to launch yourself forward if you connect with the right person.

But you can't know who that right person is. I would be lying if I said that getting a job wasn't a numbers game, because it is.

While the quality of your network matters, it's the number of reach-outs and applications you submit that will impact how many responses and real opportunities you'll get. It could be that you'll reach out to 20 people, and a few respond. But perhaps only one will offer help or refer you to someone else. This effort is still worth a shot because all it takes is one response to potentially get that job.

A few examples of how simply reaching out to a connection helped people get hired:

- A person I casually engaged with on Twitter reached out asking if I knew of any great recruiters in the London UX scene who could support a foreigner with job hunting. I had to look in my contact list, but I had worked with a couple of them in the past. This person is now living and working in London as a UX designer.
- A viewer of my YouTube channel asked if they could join my UX team. They sent a short email and told me why they'd like to work on my design team. At that time, we had several openings for designers, so their message was more than welcome. After a couple of calls, it was apparent that they were a great fit for a junior UX designer role. They were hired.
- I received a LinkedIn message asking if my company and team needed a product design contractor. I didn't have an opening that would match their seniority and skills, but I forwarded the resume to another design leader in the organisation. Long story short: they got invited to an interview.
- One of my former coworkers reached out asking if I could review his niece's portfolio as she just finished her UX bootcamp, but didn't know what to do next. I sent her some feedback and we had a back and forth about what she still needed to improve. This micro-mentorship resulted in her developing a couple of additional case studies and getting her first apprenticeship. (Do you know someone from your past workplaces or acquaintances who can give you advice? It might be worth a shot.)
- I shared a job opening on a LinkedIn board for UX strategists. A few people commented, asking about compensation, organisational culture, design maturity, challenges. Some shared the links to their resumes or simply commented, 'I'm interested'. I invited all to apply via the link and just hours later noticed that a few of the applications were the same

people who I chatted to on LinkedIn. Sometimes a simple gesture that feels small has the most significant impact. I think more highly of these candidates, knowing that they are engaged in UX communities.

The key takeaway here is that if you don't ask for something, you won't get it.

Often all you need to do is reach out to people even if you barely know them. Sometimes everything aligns - the needs, timing, opportunity scope, the skills required vs the ones you have - and you might get in.

If you're now ready to start reaching out to your connections, consider this advice:

- **Make a list of all the people you've engaged with to date**, directly or indirectly. Then mark all those who could benefit from your help, and also those who might know someone else who would. Then reach out to them individually. In your message you could recap your previous encounter(s) first, and thank them for working together. It's always a good idea to finish off by asking if they have any opportunities or know someone else who does. It's ok if you get a 'no'. You're just reconnecting to see if there's any overlap in terms of work. Even if this person doesn't have any leads right then, the very next time they do have an open opportunity that matches what you asked for, they might remember you.
- If you plan to reach out cold to any connections, **do thorough research to determine if there are suitable openings in their companies**. It would help if you also looked at what the team you're looking to join is (or could be) working on, its culture, values, etc. It's a big turn-off when candidates don't do their homework.
- Most importantly, understand that **the more senior the person, the less time they dedicate to admin tasks like reading emails** and responding to random requests. Never send a 'hi' or 'hello' and expect them to be chatty. They probably have ten meetings that day as well as plenty of other tasks. Your message needs to be clear and to the point.

- **Focus on making a connection and fostering a relationship.** Do ask for help directly but make it discreet and valuable for the other person. Connecting is about mutual benefit, not just what's in it for you.

APPLY FOR IN-HOUSE JUNIOR POSITIONS

Most junior-level designers feel stuck because they aim too high. They seek well-paid roles that require expertise and years of experience. Of course they fail to land them.

If I wanted to join an established organisation with a design function already in place, I wouldn't be too selective. At this point, you might have several months of experience solving problems, but the actual knowledge acquisition will happen in the next 2-3 years of hard work. **That's why you should apply for a design team, not a fancy company or brand.** Your goal should be to get in the door somewhere where you can learn.

Then I challenge you to consider what you should learn and add to your portfolio to grow into those better paid positions. You should think of the financial success as a side effect of you being a good designer in the first place – it's a direct translation of the value you bring to the table.

For now, don't focus too much on your exact contribution (or a lack thereof); as a growing designer, it's ok that you can't bring much value yet. Instead, stay focussed on improving yourself.

When looking for in-house junior positions, use LinkedIn, Indeed, Twitter, Google jobs search and other places. Don't just apply blindly. Aside from checking the job description, look into the company, check who the lead or senior designers are and check what they share and publish online. This will help you gauge what skillsets they care about so you can better position yourself as a good candidate.

In case you couldn't tell yet, the secret sauce to getting into UX is research.

REACH OUT TO TALENT AGENCIES AND TECH RECRUITERS

Before applying for jobs, consider if you want to work with a recruiter who specialises in UX. They could help you to infiltrate the market quicker or at least give you some constructive advice. They see countless applicants so they know exactly what hiring managers are looking for.

You might be wondering whether a recruiter would be able to find the right opportunity for you and also how you would pay them. Recruiters are usually sourced and funded by the potential employer. They get a cut on your potential salary in a specified %. It's usually in their interest to get a better deal for you, as their own earnings depend on it.

The trouble with recruiters is that it's hard to find one who can help juniors so you shouldn't rely on this as your only path to getting a job. To start, I'd recommend searching on Google and LinkedIn for talent recruitment agencies in your country and in the area you want to target. In particular, look for those who specialise in tech and UX design talent. It's even better if they have at least a handful of openings for juniors.

Alternatively, the hiring market has been shifting towards more automated ways of talent sourcing, with platforms such as Hired or Vettery (no affiliation). While most of their openings do require sizable experience, a strong portfolio could still do the talking for you as a junior candidate.

ATTEND GRADUATE AND TECH CAREER FAIRS

Just like internships, opportunities available at career fairs vary from country to country. For example, graduate programmes in the US refer to advanced studies, e.g. to attain a masters degree or a PhD. In the UK and Europe graduate programmes refer to post-graduation job opportunities where established companies interview and welcome newly graduated people into selected starter roles. These programmes might take a few years to complete, but they are not much different from a regular junior position.

In the past few years, I've seen some of the biggest companies (*Amazon, Google, Pivotal, Shell, KPMG, Deloitte, Accenture* etc.) advertise their graduate programmes, internships and other openings. Such mature organisations, often with a global reach, realise that the cheapest, most reliable investment in workforce growth is to invest in their entry-level and junior recruitment.

While rare, if you can find a career fair with multiple companies available to you, it might be the perfect opportunity for a person who's still learning and finding their footing. While there's a lot of competition for these roles, companies do try to provide graduates and juniors with the best deal.

Keep in mind that career fairs are rare and often happen once or twice yearly. It's also a big gamble that the right employer will be there advertising what's relevant to you. So in addition to attending career fairs, you could search the careers sites of big organisations to see if they offer graduate programmes.

∞

INTERVIEWS: WHAT TO EXPECT
AND PREPARE FOR

You might already know that the interview processes can throw different curveballs. It's unpredictable and you can't control every variable. This doesn't just apply to junior designer roles – the struggle is real for everyone no matter their seniority.

Don't get discouraged, though. In situations like these, I love to apply the Stoic principle of **separating things outside your control from things you can take control of**. It means that to succeed you need to focus on your strengths instead of weaknesses. Also, if you worry too much about what you can't control, the anxiety may cause you to do poorly in the interview.

A typical UX interview process will include some version of the following steps:

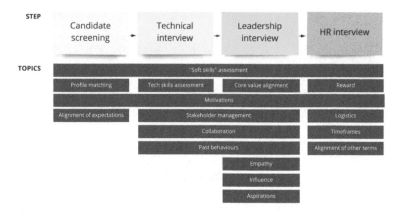

Take note of the high-level topics as I'll break those down in the following chapter. This breakdown should help you understand what hiring managers and interview teams look for, so that you can increase your chances of passing the interviews.

BEHIND THE SCENES OF EARLY CANDIDATE ASSESSMENT PROCESS

From the moment you find the right job ad and submit your application, your audience (the recruiter and the hiring manager) are involved in several different steps. These are often invisible, so before we jump into the interview how-tos, it's worth also understanding how your early applications are being assessed:

1. **You:** find a job ad, get referred by someone or otherwise apply for the UX opportunity.
2. **The recruitment manager:** reviews several applications and filters out those who are obviously unqualified. To assess this, they'll consider the applicant's experience in years, keywords that highlight specific skills, their portfolio case studies and any other items that they have agreed on with the hiring manager whom they're supporting.
3. **The hiring manager:** reviews your resume for experience, projects, skills, education and other factors.
4. **The hiring manager:** reviews your portfolio.
5. **The hiring manager:** shares their feedback with the recruitment manager. They'll share the positives, negatives and

any areas of concern. You can never know what happens in the hiring manager's mind. Their own background, self-awareness (or a lack thereof), their biases and ability to assess candidates objectively are all factors in your application that you can't influence.

6. **The recruitment manager:** shares the feedback from the hiring manager. Sadly because of a variety of reasons not every recruitment manager gets back to the applicants. However, you'll always hear back if they want to proceed with you. This is typically a phone call or email to schedule a screening call with the recruiter or the hiring manager.

7. **You:** have a short call to discuss your background, salary expectations, what you want from the role, why you're leaving your current job (if you have one). They will also take time to answer your questions. It's a good idea to always prepare some questions in advance so that you seem engaged and interested.

8. **The hiring manager and recruiter:** discuss perceived pros and cons, and decide whether to invite you for the next round of interviews.

If after this process you get a screening call, it means your portfolio, resume and other peripheral assets showed enough potential to proceed. This is a really great sign. If not, whatever you have shared was not what the interviewers were expecting. In this case, I'd recommend to always follow up to find out why.

For now let's imagine that the application was successful and the hiring team is intrigued to have a chat.

THE RECRUITER INTRO AND SCREENING CALLS

In this call, you'll be asked about your current status, salary expectations, why you want to join the company you've applied for, and other factors.

In practice, if you get called in for a screening interview, there's a high chance you'll move into the next stage. The screening calls are used to match the expectations of the company and the candidate. If you don't get invited to proceed, then you probably shared something that the recruiter didn't expect based on your application and resume. If this happens to you, follow up with the recruiter to find out why they passed on your application.

You can also reduce the chances of this happening by preparing two things in advance of the call:

Firstly, a short overview of your career in UX to date. It can be tempting to recite your resume but instead you should succinctly highlight your key achievements that are relevant to the role you're interviewing for. As you wrap up, you can hint at what *you* want from the role.

Secondly, consider your salary expectations. Research salary ranges for the seniority of the role you're applying for, the area, and the company. Being out of sync on salary expectations is a key reason why people don't get invited to the next stage. Typically, hiring managers are looking for a specific skill set and seniority level within a certain salary range. Bigger organisations can also have specific salary bands that hiring managers can't influence or change easily, even when they otherwise like the candidate.

My final advice for screening calls is to avoid over-preparing. People who interview candidates all the time can immediately tell if what you say is scripted or over-rehearsed. It's much better to stumble and sound human than fake it and appear disingenuous. As long as you are clear in your communication (don't waffle or try to sound more experienced than you are), you will be fine.

After the screening call, you're in the proper interviewing phase where you interact directly with the hiring manager and other team members. Next, I'll go over what this phase entails.

TECHNICAL INTERVIEWS

Technical interviews are very important at the beginning of your UX career. Depending on the organisation, this could be one interview or multiple rounds and your capabilities will be assessed in different ways.

Some general activities that make up technical interviews include:

The portfolio review

You will be asked to walk the interviewers through your work. This is the most critical part of any interview as both your technical and soft skills will be assessed simultaneously.

For the walk-through, use the case study that's the most relevant to the role and be very honest about your considerations, compromises and learnings. It's ok to say that you'd do something differently the next time or that not everything went as planned. **If you get to the technical interview, then the hiring team thinks you have enough potential** to do the work. Think of this interview not as a test but as an activity to contextualise what you're showing in your portfolio.

Therefore, it's more important that you know the story of your case study and can walk people through it in a concise and compelling manner. Practice so you don't drone on for ages.

The UX skills assessment

The hiring team wants to gauge your UX acumen. They do this during portfolio reviews and during other discussions when they ask about your UX skills and processes.

To assess acumen as a hiring manager, I always want to understand a candidate's reasoning for the decisions made in the design process, especially if they seem questionable to me. Know that it's not your decisions that are being judged but rather how you arrived at them. So you should be able to provide a rationale for why you chose to do personas, how you'd use specific persona information to inform your work, why you did a particular research activity, or how you planned the research.

The key is to help the hiring team understand why you did what you did.

Aside from direct questions, your UX skills might be assessed through some of the following activities as well:

Active participatory assessments and whiteboarding exercises

Many companies employ whiteboarding exercises and project-like roleplaying to assess candidates. You will most likely get a challenge brief then be asked to think out loud or use a whiteboard to solve the challenge. You might also need to work with other people on the brief, typically from the team you'd be working with as a UX designer or researcher.

I'm not a fan of this method as it's synthetic and staged. It doesn't mimic how UX is actually done. Even if it tries to simulate real problem-solving scenarios, all it does is test your ability to cope with scope and sort-of-work with strangers.

The hiring team is trying to see how you reason, work with others, and approach problems on demand, so just go along with it and do your best.

Meet the team

You'll usually get to meet at least one of your potential teammates during the interview process. Some companies run several rounds of interviews in order to have more teammates interview and assess the candidate.

This is another activity which I'm not a fan of because most people are unskilled at interviewing others objectively. The teams that let unqualified people interview others often hire people they like or immediately get along with, rather than people who are qualified for the job.

That said, if you are interviewed by your potential peers, just be yourself. You can't control their biases so just be humble, honest and respectful.

Also use this as an opportunity to ask questions about the company culture and teamwork so that you know if the role will fit your needs.

Take-home assignments

This is another activity that's frowned upon by most hiring managers who respect their applicant's time and don't make them work for free. Thankfully it's becoming passé.

A take-home assignment is when a company sends you a lengthier assignment to complete in your own time, outside of other interviews. My advice to juniors who ask how they should approach this exercise is to commit to it only if it's worth your time.

To know if it's worth your time, assess the benefit vs cost of time spent.
For example:

1. Could the assignment become your next case study, or
2. Is it worth it since you really really, really want to work for this particular company, or
3. Does it take less than a couple of hours of your time and ties into the 1st point?

If you can't justify the assignment with any of these 3 reasons, then I'd advise you to be very careful with it.

I appreciate that it's unrealistic for you to reject the assignment and still proceed through the process so I have another suggestion for you: **compromise**. Instead of doing the assignment on your own, propose to run a UX workshop (to frame or reframe the problem), or run a white-board exercise with the design and product team.

While in the beginning of your career you have to compromise more, as you gain experience and change jobs you'll soon need to figure out how to respect your own time. I have a video just on this topic: https://bit.ly/UXtakeHome.

∞

SOFT SKILLS AND LEADERSHIP INTERVIEWS

Most companies make an effort to ask specific questions relating to their values. Their goal is to assess whether you'd fit the organisational culture and work to their core values.

Prepare for these questions. Research the company's career site to understand what their values are. Even though exact verbiage can vary, there are some core values that all companies look for in a candidate:

Empathy and other social factors
You will be asked about and assessed on collaboration, empathy, and

similar social factors. Specifically, you might be asked about challenges you faced when working with a team or specific individuals. You'll also be assessed on how you approach understanding and helping other people.

Ensure that you answer these questions without complaining about others and instead communicate how you work with teams and handle interpersonal challenges.

Stakeholder management and influence

You'll need to demonstrate the ability to influence business representatives and drive user-centricity even when it wasn't welcome. How do you affect people in general? What techniques and methods do you use to take people on the journey? How do you challenge or work with people who might be more senior than you?

One memorable question I received when applying for a senior UX designer role went like this: "Can you tell us about a time when a senior stakeholder requested a digital solution design (e.g., an app), and how did you handle it?"

One incorrect answer would be to say that you'd jump in and design the UI for that app right away.

The correct answer is to first understand why they want that digital solution, then advocate for UX research to prove that it's truly needed. The interview is, again, trying to understand your thinking in how you'd handle the situation.

Self awareness

You'll be assessed on this throughout the interview stages, as the interviewers will evaluate how well you understand your own actions and the thinking behind them.

Still there are also common questions used specifically to assess your self-awareness. These questions are about any of the following:

1. What are your weaknesses or areas you're working to improve on?

2. What are your strengths? What do you usually contribute to projects?
3. Where do you see yourself in X years?
4. … in hindsight, how different would your actions be? What would you have done differently if there hadn't been any limits?

And many more.

Consider what you would say in response to each of these difficult questions so you are more prepared to answer them when they inevitably come up.

Leadership

Juniors tend to think that it's the only seasoned designers with teams under them who lead and have authority. This is a misconception. We choose to lead whether or not there's any following. In the early years of your career, when you don't have a team reporting to you, you can show authority and leadership values in three ways:

- How you lead and motivate yourself
- How you lead the UX process and champion it regardless of whether anyone else in the company cares
- Through thought leadership and influence

The more senior you get, the more important it becomes to display leadership values.

Personal management

Not to be mistaken with leadership, personal management is how you hold yourself in communities and spaces you are a part of. Hiring teams will always want to understand how competent and motivated you are, whether you're engaged with the industry, and if you can get things done well and in reasonable time.

Many junior designers think time is the important factor so they focus on speed of completing deliverables. Quality matters more than speed. The latter will come with more experience, as you'll be seasoned enough to act faster.

IN SUMMARY

What you need to demonstrate at this early stage in your career is that you are applying for the right reasons and that you want to contribute. To do this, showcase how you did things with agency. To prove your soft skills, be ready to talk through specific examples and their outcomes.

You might think that you don't have any examples to reinforce your points, but you always do: consider your school, studies, bootcamps, side jobs, freelance gigs, and any other situations where you had to practice your soft skills.

Naturally, the more UX-related the examples are, the more likely your answer is to resonate with the hiring team, but it is valuable to be able to spin any past event into an experience that's useful and relevant to the job you're applying for.

INTERVIEW WITH HR / PEOPLE OPS AND OFFER NEGOTIATIONS

If you've gotten this far in the hiring process, chances are you'll get an offer! To ensure that this final interview goes smoothly, prepare for the following three questions.

Your salary expectations

Depending on your location you might have covered this during the screening call early on[1]. Sometimes salary expectations need to be revisited after later interviews (depending on whether you seemed more or less competent than expected). Usually, the company will make a salary offer for you to respond to.

The best way to respond to a salary offer or when you're asked what salary you expect is to give an expected range along with a thought-out reason behind it. For example, I would expect an interviewee to say, "Given the current (local) market rates and my strong skills as compared to the market averages, I'm looking for 20-30k *vaexperience bucks*.". Former FBI hostage negotiator Chris Voss (who has done a fair amount of bidding in negotiations[2]) advises to list the salary you actually expect as the bottom of your range.

The range you give needs to be reasonable, however. I've witnessed junior candidates ask for senior salaries and it just got them rejected. If you haven't done the research already for the screening call, then now is the time to consider what salary range is appropriate for the role, seniority, region, industry and any other relevant factor.

Once you learn UX and progress your career, you'll be able to call the shots on salary increases fairly quickly. As I've said before, for now I'd advise you to focus on picking the right learning environment first and to ask for a reasonable salary that you would be happy with.

Your start date

If you're applying for your first job, your start date will likely be as soon as possible. That's great.

However, when people switch from one job to another they often want to take some time off in between which pushes out their start date. If you're in this situation, consider if pushing out your start date is worth doing.

Not every team manager has the luxury of being able to wait months for a candidate to start. That's especially true of junior roles that already have high competition.

It's fine if you still decide to push out your start date, just be aware of whether this could put the job opportunity at risk and harm your long-term career.

Your reason to join the organisation

HR people sometimes revisit topics you already discussed in previous interview stages. For example, they'll commonly ask questions to assess your core values, leadership and empathy. It's unlikely that they'll dive deep into these areas, as they're just doing a final sweep for any red flags but it doesn't hurt to be prepared anyway.

∞

1. The salary negotiation process varies by region and country. For example, during the editing process of this book I discovered that in the US salary discussions are kept to the very last moment, and usually candidates have no say in this. This is the opposite to what you'd experience in European markets, where candidates need to state their salary expectations during application, screening call and then negotiate in the last stages of the interviews when an offer is made. Act accordingly to your region and situation.

2. I highly recommend his book, *Never split the difference: negotiating as if your life depended on it.*

INTERVIEWS: HOW TO BE EFFECTIVE AND PERFORM YOUR BEST

We've established that you need to be prepared to answer specific questions. On top of that, there are some general heuristics you can use in interviews to answer any question more effectively, regardless of the topic.

REFERENCE EVIDENCE IN YOUR ANSWERS

For any question you get, reference a relevant example from the past to help answer it. You should have some examples of technical and interpersonal challenges ready before you interview so you can remember them on the spot.

Having examples matters because the interviewer doesn't actually want to hear how you did something. They want to see that you can talk about a problem and the skills or steps you used to get to a solution. To help you communicate that, refer to the storytelling skills I shared as they can help you to better frame answers and evidence statements.

Naturally, many juniors struggle to come up with great examples because they are early in their journeys. If you can't think of an example, simulate a scenario of what you would do in the case you're asked about.

For example, you could say, "*While I haven't done that before, if I could do [example], I'd do it as follows [insert an example of what you think would be appropriate to do]...*"

Remember, it's always better to show self-awareness by admitting to not having experience or skill in a particular area than trying to lie.

ASK QUESTIONS TO UNDERSTAND THE CONTEXT

If you don't fully understand a question, don't wing your answer. It's ok for a question to be too vague to you, as you don't know the ins and outs of the organisation yet. That's why it's ok to ask for clarification.

Don't forget that it's not just you who is being interviewed here. You are also interviewing the recruiter and the hiring manager to assess if the company is the right fit for you. Don't be afraid to ask questions.

If they're not willing to answer your questions (which has happened to me when a hiring team refused to have a two-way conversation), then that could be a red flag. This may be a culture in which curiosity is not valued, or they believe that their way is the only way.

ASK QUESTIONS TO UNDERSTAND THE ORGANISATION AND THE POSITION BETTER

Most organisations will give you time and opportunity to ask your questions throughout the process. Sometimes you'll be able to just simply have a chat, other times they might time box it.

A rule of thumb: always have a question up your sleeve. When candidates don't ask any questions it signals lack of interest. So ask away!

I recommend to ask questions about:

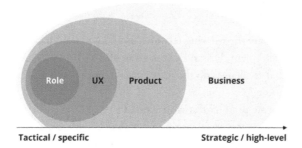

* **The role you're applying for**
* **The UX capability**
* **The product capability**
* **The business and the wider organisation**

Some of my favourite go-to questions on these topics are:

Role specific:

* What are the key expectations of the role?
* What skillset will be necessary to succeed in this role?
* What are the expectations for the first 3 months in the role?
* Is the role brand new or replacing someone in an existing project?

UX specific:

* What's the current team structure? How is the team operating in terms of supporting the business initiatives?
* What do they expect this UX role will bring to the table? What change are they seeking?
* How would they describe the design maturity in the team and the wider org currently?
* What are the key UX team challenges they are trying to address?
* What's the vision for the team development?
* Quoting what you already know: "I've noticed that in the job ad you say…" - how is that currently done in the team?

Product specific:

- What are the working relationships between product management, UX and engineering like?
- What challenges do the teams have in terms of their ways of working?
- How are product teams structured?
- What are the key areas that UX can help with the most?
- How are product decisions made right now? Where do the insights come from to make more strategic decisions?
- What are some example outcomes or measures that product and UX are tracking?

Business and organisation specific:

- Can they share any high-level strategic developments or goals?
- How is the UX capability viewed in the wider org?
- Quoting a competitor or highlighting their offering features: What are they looking to improve on in the next few years?

Make sure to prepare enough questions to cover at least 20 minutes of the conversation. I usually recommend people prepare at least 10 questions and write them down to use in the interviews. It's ok to bring out a notepad and read out of it if need be. A lot of experienced designers (myself included) will do just that.

Furthermore, don't be afraid to ask questions on the fly based on where the conversation is going. This will demonstrate your comprehension and engagement; the two factors that are most important for building an instant connection with a stranger.

DEMONSTRATE AWARENESS ABOUT THE ORGANISATION

I interviewed a candidate who applied for a position in business area A, but then during the interview they talked about business area B. If you are interviewing for a role on the internal tools team but talk about the public-facing customer app, it becomes clear very quickly that you might not be a good match as you didn't do enough research.

Prepare and spend just a little bit more time than necessary to understand what the company is about and what the role entails. To form a better understanding of both things, you could read employee reviews on Glassdoor, research social media posts from the company, and check the company's news bulletins.

SHOW SOME PASSION TO BOOST YOUR POTENTIAL

While you shouldn't fake the enthusiasm for UX or the position, you need to show enough passion and drive.

In the eyes of the hiring team, passion is synonymous with the potential you have to be a great designer and employee. This is why people with *good* portfolios will be picked over people with *great* portfolios if the latter display little passion.

The easiest way to show passion is to show interest. Ask questions to show that you're trying to understand the interviewers and the organisation. Tie that understanding into showing how you could be valuable to them.

Generally, if you can demonstrate passion around 1) **why you like UX**, 2) **what it means to you**, and 3) **why you're interviewing with this company in the first place** – you'll be more likely to get in.

BUILD A CONNECTION WITH THE HIRING TEAM

Ask the hiring team about their own experiences, what they need help with or what challenges they are facing. If you're interviewed by people outside of UX (such as product managers or engineers), ask them how they interact with the role you're applying for or what they expect from it. Ultimately, a company is made up of individuals, and by appealing to individuals, you will have a better chance.

You won't have enough time to build a relationship within minutes, and that's fine. You just want the hiring team to walk away from the conversation thinking that they want to work with you. (And you should walk away thinking the same about them.)

ADDRESS ANY RESERVATION THE HIRING TEAM HAS

This is a killer, albeit controversial move that I've employed for as long as I remember. Here's how to do it properly: when wrapping things up, one of the final questions you should ask is if the interviewers still have any reservations about hiring you.

You see, people will always have concerns, however small. Your goal here is to nip those concerns in the bud while you still have control.

The hiring team will often respond with some feedback for you to consider. You might not have enough time to unpack and respond to it fully, but even asking about it shows that you care. It signals self-awareness. It shows that you want to connect and problem solve there and in that moment. That will be taken as the ultimate example of you taking ownership.

People assume and hope for the best even if they know that the interviewers will always have something on their minds. Next time you interview, make sure to lead and stand out from the crowd by taking ownership.

There's nothing better than a simple question: "*Do you have any reservations over what we discussed?*", or "*Is there anything I can quickly address that you have concerns about?*"

∞

WHAT DO TO IF YOU'RE APPLYING BUT NOT GETTING ANYWHERE

At this point it's essential to state that every designer faces rejection in their careers. However, entry-level and junior candidates can get discouraged and give up more quickly than most because they haven't yet experienced the harsh realities of the job market. Understand that job hunting is difficult for everyone, regardless of their role and seniority level.

You should accept now that you will be rejected. There's so many factors influencing your application that you can't control. **Once you accept that there are factors out of your control and that rejection is inevitable, you can put them aside and double down on the factors that you can control.**

THINGS THAT ARE IN YOUR CONTROL

In the first chapter of this book, I described what factors keep candidates from entering the experience design market:

- **They are looking for a silver bullet**
- **They lack a fundamental understanding of UX**
- **They mistake UI for UX**
- **They lack commercial experience**
- **They listen to yay and nay-sayers too much**
- **They are too picky**

- **They focus on short-term opportunities**
- **They have poor portfolio case studies**

But if you diligently followed this book so far, you also know that you have the power to address all of these factors yourself:

They are looking for a silver bullet	They must grow into UX over the years, but start working now
They lack a fundamental understanding of UX	They need to ignore the noise and trust the proven process
They often mistake UI for UX	They must focus on user research as the bedrock of UX
They lack commercial experience	They need to do their own projects that can lead to commercial projects and experience
They listen to yay and nay-sayers too much	They need to find better mentors and communities that support growth
They are too picky	They need to focus on learning
They focus on short-term opportunities	They need to define goals, always think and act with long term outcomes in mind
They have poor portfolio case studies	They must apply all of the above principles and work on their portfolios tirelessly

Don't give up after the first failure or a lack of response. Through repeated practice and given enough time, you'll fill the gaps and form a strong base of skills and user-centred thinking. You will become a more effective designer.

THINGS THAT AREN'T IN YOUR CONTROL

There are things that you can rarely influence, if at all:

One position – hundreds of applicants

Just the other day, I saw a job opening for a junior UX designer on LinkedIn, and it already had 211 applicants! These numbers would be typical for very desirable FAANG jobs – *Facebook, Amazon, Apple, Netflix, Google* and other overhyped tech firms, but not so much for an average, unknown firm. It's a harsh reality check for everyone in the UX industry, as this competitive landscape is here to stay.

Having said that, what's in your control is demonstrating the evidence that can help you stand out from the crowd of applicants. That's why the QUALITY of your work and UX skills is so important to boost your potential and get hired.

You don't know who you're competing against

You will never know the actual calibre of other applicants and whether they are better than you. The market is saturated with unqualified and unconvincing candidates.

If you get rejected during the interviewing stage, you'll never know what influenced the company to drop your application. Even if they give you feedback or say they selected another candidate, you can't know what that candidate demonstrated that you did not.

The solution here is simple: let go of thinking about the other applicants; focus on yourself and make your application stand out by following everything this book has covered so far.

The issue of being a runner-up

Have you ever heard of the idea that Olympic athletes would rather win bronze than silver? Making the 3rd place means reaching the podium and leaving other competitors behind – a massive win. Meanwhile, achieving 2nd and getting silver symbolises a failure to win – you're the first person to lose.

You will experience this same runner-up effect in your job search. Each opening has only one gold medal; there are always going to be runner-ups and people who fail at the last stage.

Imagine interviewing for hours, across days and weeks, and then finding out that you weren't picked to proceed further. Only the hiring managers know who you're compared against and by what criteria. These comparisons can be tough and unfair.

For example, when I have an opening in one of my design teams, I often get multiple candidates who I'd hire instantly, if only I had additional positions available. As a hiring manager, I am constrained by budgets, headcount limitations, projects that need only one designer, and other factors.

Inevitably, hiring managers like myself must turn down quality candidates, and one of them might be you.

The hiring process can take a long time

Depending on the organisation type, size, location, project and role timing and the urgency for talent, the hiring process could take days, weeks or even months. In the past, I've seen several openings at FAANG that have been around for over a year—granted this is usually the case for high-stakes, senior roles.

Ultimately, it could take you months to hear back, if at all! If you get ghosted, it's worth noting that companies have a lot of departments, teams and cultures – just because you had a bad experience with a company for one role, it doesn't mean you'd be dealing with the same people if you applied again down the line.

I once had to convince my mentee to re-apply for a company they were avoiding because of a terrible past interview experience. The new role was in a different part of the organisation. To their surprise, they found the experience better the second time around and even got a job offer this time.

The moral of the story is that it's always worth keeping an open mind about the hiring process, as you never know who is involved or what might have changed since your last encounter.

GIVING UP WAY TOO EARLY

The single biggest complaint I get from designers at all seniority levels is that they might have applied for countless openings but haven't heard back. Because it's so common, it's crucial to keep hammering this point again and again until it becomes something you're not surprised to experience anymore.

The job market is a fragmented, brutal place where even the most experienced designers might struggle to find their next opportunity. You need to be ready for this.

To help adjust your expectations around rejections and waiting times, I'll walk you through my own job transition from a few years ago. Bear in mind that at this point I had a decade of experience and was looking for a management role.

To clarify, I wasn't then and I'm not now an expert in all things UX. For one, it's practically impossible to develop expertise in all of the UX disciplines, and for two, I am a professional who has faced many challenges and has grown into a strong UX designer, design leader, and team manager over many years.

Landing the right role still took me a few months and my whole journey looked like this:

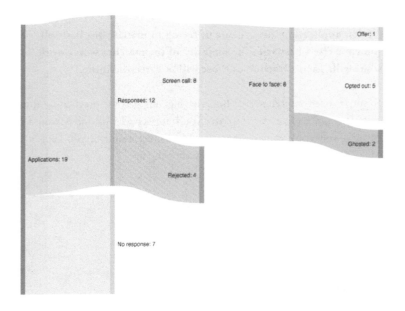

What stands out to you?

Perhaps that:

1. I got only one offer?
2. I opted out from five opportunities voluntarily?
3. For the bulk of opportunities I was either rejected or got no response?

The reality here is that it's hard to find an opportunity that will challenge you and allow you to grow. Regardless of your seniority level. On top of that, you need to also consider that hiring managers have their own unique challenges and needs. Most of the time you won't be able to tell exactly what type of skills they are truly after. They could also be running against tight timeframes and budget constraints with very little wiggle room.

That is why, having interviewed with countless of companies over the years, I'm no longer surprised by such outcomes when I need to apply for new positions.

Recently, one of my viewers commented that finding a job in UX is like dating and I couldn't agree more:
 Job applications are a game of trying to match your best self with someone else's best self. The majority of the matches won't work, but some will. Then a fraction of those will be career-defining.

If you've been applying and interviewing but getting nowhere – don't stop. It could be that the employer you interviewed with today would be entirely wowed by your skills next week or next month if you kept at it. Make sure to maintain focus and keep showing up.

Keep on, keeping on.

∞

PART 4

WHAT TO DO ONCE YOU GET THERE (THE BONUS PART)

CHAPTER 7

BUILD FORWARD MOMENTUM

"The professional arms himself with patience, not only to give the stars time to align in his career, but to keep himself from flaming out in each individual work."

STEVEN PRESSFIELD

If you've gotten this far, you've unlocked a bonus section that contains a few essays to help you as you continue your UX career. While these essays are aimed at beginners, they'll be relevant to all UX designers out there.

Before you get too far into this section, you should apply all of the advice I've shared in previous chapters first: learn UX, practice, collect the evidence and land that UX gig you're after. You should be in a pretty good place once you've done all of that.

If you're not there yet flip back to the actual phase you're in. Getting into UX will take time, so spend it well on each step.

Once you land that first UX role, you'll invariably face the first bouts of challenges that I only hinted at in the chapter titled 'Firstly, who is a UX designer?" Those challenges include:

Interpersonal issues: You may be dealing with difficult stakeholders, an unsupportive project team, general miscommunication, project misalignment or a lack of trust.

These issues could be caused by bad leadership, a fragmented culture, by specific individuals who are hard to work with or by your own unpreparedness. While you can't predict or influence the culture easily, what's in your control is your attitude, behaviours and skills.

The employer fundamentally misunderstands UX: It could be that the company didn't invest that much into its user-centricity before you started. Perhaps design gets the shorter end of the stick.

Sometimes it might be about budgets; other times, about a misunderstanding of what UX stands for. Commonly, they don't understand why user research is so essential. I've been part of many firms where design was an afterthought, and sadly until you reach the leadership level, you can't easily shape attitudes or drive organisational change for the better.

Forgetting business goals: New designers tend to focus on user needs but often forget the underlying business goals. Back when I started out, I naively thought that a kickass UI which delights users was the only thing that mattered.

I now know that all solutions and features are useless if they don't produce value for all the parties involved and if they don't contribute to the business' bottom line. It's what you got hired for; to deliver value for both the users and the business.

While you don't have to sell your soul, keep in mind that UX is expensive (though not doing UX is even more so), and you should contribute to business outcomes, just like any other employee.

Personal management issues: Many will face an inability to manage themselves or their time in their first role.

To address this you will need to learn the appropriate cadence; how to pace yourself to be productive without burning out. Often juniors can overcommit in order to demonstrate their value but this isn't sustainable.

To perform well sustainably, you'll need to manage your workload, set clear expectations and work as a team.

Sadly, but not surprisingly you wouldn't learn about any of these challenges in a typical UX course or bootcamp.

In the following essays, I'll break down the above challenges and equip you with a simple set of tools, ideas and methods to deal with them. Remember to practice these methods to get better; the key to growth is repetition.

COLLABORATE

What a lot of new designers and researchers get wrong is thinking that their job is to take a brief, go away, and come back with a clever design. This can't be further from the truth.

When you research and design in isolation, it's harder for people to buy into your insights, ideas or solution prototypes.

Instead it's important that you see user experience design as a team sport, especially at the junior level. You must bring others on the journey with you even if they show resistance or you won't be able to deliver the solutions you think users need.

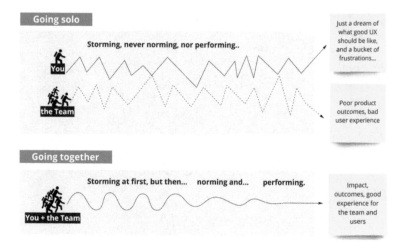

Bringing others along can mean engaging with the business stakeholders, playing back findings from user research, influencing the product strategy to become user-centric. It can also include running research workshops, collaborating with developers, and many other activities that rely on more than one hero to deliver a great user experience.

Yet collaboration is rarely taught. In school or bootcamps, we acquire experience by solving problems in staged social environments but in isolation. So when we enter the workforce, we continue to work that way. UX might have been your sole responsibility in school, but that's not true in the world of work, and being a solo player won't help you in your career. In the words of Cal Newport, what got you here (to your first job) won't get you there (up the career ladder)[1].

From a hiring manager's perspective, a candidate who has collaborated with a client, user, developer or any other stakeholder will always trump another who hasn't.

---

1. *What Got You Here Won't Get You There* is a book by Marshall Goldsmith, which I recommend to any developing designer. This book unpacks the key interpersonal issues and skills people need to work with others. However, the actual phrase can describe any phase of learning and progressing - the skills you learn and master will become a baseline and you should always aim to learn something new that will make you more effective.

BE PRAGMATIC

While the most common issue with designers is that they skip proper user research, there are also those idealists who think that UX is the most important factor for a project's success.

Such romanticised views, while necessary for creativity, will hold you back in business. You need both creative idealism and its opposite, pragmatism, to be a good UX researcher or designer.

In your day-to-day you'll be marrying the pre-existing business goals and UX insights. You'll have to reflect not just on how to solve users' needs but also how to deliver value to the business and its stakeholders. Usually this means that your role is to reduce costs, increase profits, or both through a better experience.

The experience is not the end goal. The business bottom line is. If not for the business' need you wouldn't have a UX job in the first place.

UX designers are only invited to help solve problems because the business needs to achieve its bottom line.

When you take on a project you need to connect customer (or user) behaviour change with tangible business outcomes in order to add value.

Having the business acumen to be able to measure and communicate the benefits of UX is key to your long term success.

In the chapter about the streamlined design methods I introduced Design Thinking which can help you marry pragmatism and idealism well. You can use the human-centred design framework to find synergy between desirability (what the user wants), viability (business outcomes) and feasibility (technology limits):

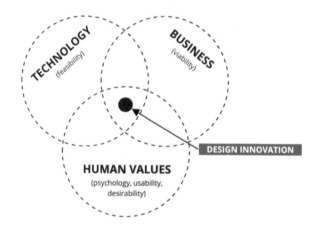

Suppose you want to do justice to customers by delivering a delightful user experience. In that case, you must also consider if that experience is possible from a tech standpoint (feasibility) and most likely readjust the end solution to be delivered in a cost-effective way that boosts revenue for the business (viability).

While tech and business dependencies might not be part of your job officially, you'll have to consider them anyway in order to deliver good UX. Aside from delivery, there's two other reasons why you should invest time in understanding the business and the tech viewpoints.

The first is that doing so is the only way you can climb the ladder into design leadership positions. The proverbial seat at the table that designers have recently been invited to take alongside product and engineering is something that can only be 'unlocked' through holistic and pragmatic ways of doing design work. You will need to boost your business acumen and tech know-how to do both.

The second is understanding that UX as a role is a change management role at its core - you will join firms to bring their attention back to user needs. Product strategist Daniel Engelberg hit the nail on the head with this post[1]:

"A lot of UX people don't realise what they're getting into. They just want to do UX. But they quickly discover half the battle is being allowed to do it. Organisations don't realise they need to change to support UX. And UX people don't realise they're stepping into a change management role..."

He also suggests focusing on the things that are truly in your control, over those you can only influence remotely:

"So the best policy is to slowly change the things you have access to: organisational processes and information structures. Once those changes are in place, values might change gradually on their own, without resistance."

Another framework that can help you be pragmatic is a decision making model such as the one developed by Kate Aronowitz (Design Partner at GV, formerly Google Ventures[2]). She sets out how designers should prioritise their work, starting with the user like so:

As the priorities and focus goes, I wholeheartedly agree that it's a great framework that shows what UX designers should care about the most. However, you will often be the only person in the room who cares about the user and their real needs, so truly prioritising the user in any solution could become challenging.

To get business and tech to buy into the solution, you have to include their needs as well. That's why I'd argue that the actual distribution of factors you should consider when making design decisions should start with the business. The user is still your key priority, which is why I made it the biggest block, but you should start by understanding the business first:

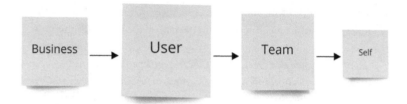

- **The first thing to do:** understand the business goals, success criteria for the business, project, etc.
- **Second, but clearly the most important thing for you to do:** understand users, their lives, challenges, needs and opportunities to help them achieve their goals in a meaningful way, etc.
- **Third:** the team's wellbeing and morale, operational standards, team development, business development to land more opportunities, design maturity, etc.
- **Lastly, fourth:** your personal interests. Including your needs, career progression, personal development, feelings, etc.

The self is clearly the last and the smallest item in this framework. This is for two reasons: 1) if you focus on the most important things first, the score takes care of itself, 2) personal interests are usually driven by ego, and ego harms collaboration that is so crucial to the UX field.

Starting with the business goals (with the help of the above two frameworks) has transformed my career. At first, it helped me have a more significant impact at work which marked my transition from an individual contributor to a strategist. Then it also made me a better team player as I started focussing on the needs of my design team first, rather than my own. This, finally, marked my transition to a design leader.

∞

1. Daniel Engelberg's rationale on what you must consider: https://bit.ly/ConsiderUXWork
2. You can read more about Kate Aronowitz's rationale in this great Medium article "Who sets your priorities?": https://bit.ly/DesignPriorities

KEEP BUILDING YOUR
RELATIONSHIPS

Ask any design leader these days about the importance of having a solid network of connections, and you will receive the same answer: it's crucial for your long-term success.

Connections can also be key to landing jobs. For example, a recent survey[1] into job searching discovered that 85% of jobs are filled through networking. Of course, this high percentage combines both direct and indirect referrals but still it's clear that having a meaningful connection can open up opportunities. In my own experience, most job opportunities I've taken came from someone I knew.

Yet while we understand that fostering a professional network matters, networking is the last thing junior designers would focus on. They're too busy honing their research and design skills, and doing everything else described in this book. It's good to focus on those things first but you shouldn't forget to connect with others.

You don't have to go out of your way and reach out to every suitable person. That's what made me hate networking because it felt transactional and dishonest. It's also pointless because those weak connections won't remember you when there's an opportunity they could share with you.

The advice I was given was to take the opposite approach: **Seek to learn from others instead of connecting for connection's sake.**

Although obvious, this is a less common approach because it requires you to be humble, curious and open. It's also not as tangible as traditional networking where you can count the business cards or LinkedIn connections you've made to feel a sense of achievement. But it's a lot more effective.

In terms of where and how to best network, you'll find different opportunities. Let's break them down and discuss how to approach each one to make the most of it.

ATTEND LOCAL INDUSTRY MEETUPS

Every city that is mid-size or larger, almost anywhere in the world, will have a buzzing tech hub, and usually one or several design communities.

While design communities are the most relevant to your journey, don't limit yourself to them alone. You should consider joining other industry meetups as well such as tech or psychology. You'll be surprised by how inspiring such events can be.

They can also be rewarding. Through non-design specific events you could meet people who'd benefit from your UX expertise or you can practice how to market yourself and your skills when talking to them. Even if they work in a totally different area of the business, if you make a meaningful connection they could get back to you months or years into the future to let you know about a UX opportunity. I've met many people hiring for UX designers at events not specific to design.

As for design-specific events, these are great to meet like-minded specialists, exchange ideas, challenges, or to give a talk on your recent case study. When I was still a junior in UX, I used to go to at least one meetup a week. It was my goal to build up a network of meaningful connections by joining a group of people in the same boat. This type of commitment helped me build a lot of confidence, overcome impostor syndrome, and build a network that I still benefit from today.

You can google or search on Meetups.com for events in your vicinity. Often such events are held in the evenings, so you can join them after a work day.

∞

START YOUR OWN LOCAL UX COMMUNITY/MEETUP

If you can't find a like-minded group or there isn't much of a tech scene where you are, then you could create your own community. I know this might be a big ask, especially since you're still trying to find your feet in the UX field. However, think of this effort as another effective way to learn, not just an attempt to build your network.

Firstly, creating a community or event for junior UX designers will require you to organise and manage it which will help you build important skills.

Secondly, you'll be able to add new skills and experience to your resume in addition to building a network. Any designer who has proven organisational, facilitation and people skills will always outrank someone who has only designed and worked in isolation.

Thirdly, running a meetup covering a speciality like UX will make you a thought leader or at least a credible persona with the gravitas which can help you build a meaningful network.

Most entry-level designers think that it takes a lot of effort to start and run these communities. Of course, it does. That's the whole point. You don't need me to tell you that everything worth pursuing in life will require a lot of effort – you know this already if you started your journey into UX. What's worth keeping in mind, though, is that to begin with, you don't need to go overboard with your communities.

To start, all you need to do is register as an organiser on Meetup.com, create a group with a good description, invite some friends and make a recurring event you can run consistently.

Perhaps you'll run the first set of meetups in a local cafe around the table as a chat about design. Maybe you'll want to reach out to local businesses to sponsor your meetup by providing a location for your event. You can plan your event however it makes the most sense for your location and the size of the group.

Don't forget that there's no pressure in running this every week. It could just be a monthly gathering, or you could even hold the event online.

∞

JOIN UX NETWORKING ORGANISATIONS

The passive and easy way to network is to join an existing, established UX organisation. Depending on your needs, you can find several unofficial organisations; these might be as simple as a discussion board.

Some of these will be free while others will require you to pay a membership fee. I'd recommend first exhausting your free choices and only later joining programs where you must be a paying member.

One final word of caution here is that most free groups are full of UI design that labels itself as UX. Research communities before you join them to make sure they will be helpful to you.

LinkedIn groups

You could join LinkedIn groups dedicated to UX. To start, search in LinkedIn for "user experience," "experience design," or similar keywords, and then filter by groups. You should aim to join some more prominent groups, as well as small groups that are still developing. You want to find the sweet middle ground where people are active, they freely share their experiences and give feedback to others.

To give you a few options, these are some groups I've benefited from in the past and also heard my mentees get value out of:

- UX/HCI Researchers: https://bit.ly/UXHCIgroup
- Interaction Design Association: https://bit.ly/IDAgroup
- User experience group: https://bit.ly/UXgroup
- BetterUX Community: https://bit.ly/BetterUXgroup
- UX Strategy: https://bit.ly/UXStrategygroup

International UX organisations

For example, there's the User Experience Professionals Association (UXPA) or Interaction Design Association (IxDA). These two have impressive clout and a minimal fee. They also provide an already existing extensive network of designers who run events, conferences and knowledge-sharing sessions.

Some organisations you have to pay to join will also have a free-to-join community on a social network you might already use. I'd advise you to assess the free community first before paying for a membership.

Unofficial organisations, communities and networks

In addition to formal channels, you should also engage informally with other designers. There's Slack channels, Reddit design boards, UX troubleshooting platforms, Discord servers, and other groups that are just a Google search away. The more specific you are with the search term, the more likely you are to find the right community.

I've already mentioned our Discord community - the Design Squad. You can freely join it via the following link: https://bit.ly/designsquadux. I made this space so people like you can connect, ask for advice, share their learnings, helpful material, tools, and generally build their design network.

As an action step, I'd recommend joining at least one networking organisation. Make sure to focus on learning and contributing. Help others first then ask for advice of your own. If you do this right you'll form relationships and the network of like-minded people will grow organically.

But wait, what if you can't find a community to join? Create your own! That's more challenging and it takes time to get traction when you start from nothing, but it could help you foster an even stronger network. To help you gain traction, create your community on a platform where UX'ers or junior designers already gather. Even if your community has fewer members, it could become more helpful or more active than communities with hundreds of thousands of members.

If you're still unsure where to start, UX'ers tend to love gathering on dedicated Slack channels, Reddit, Discord, Linkedin, and even Facebook. The aim here is to create a networking channel on a platform with enough junior designers to get traction.

∞

OTHER (GOOD AND NOT SO GREAT) NETWORKING OPTIONS

Conferences (preferably in person)

Conferences are not my number one choice for networking, especially if they are remote/online. They don't allow for serendipity or contextual conversations that would happen organically. For many reasons, this is not an ideal way to make lasting connections. Rather, conferences are good for exposing yourself to fresh ideas so you can walk away feeling inspired or having learnt something new.

Webinars

Most webinars these days are time-wasting, covert sales pitches providing minimum value to hook you into buying a product or service. It's a poor choice for networking as it's usually one speaker talking to the attendees, with no ability for the attendees to talk to each other. No thanks.

Live streams

A livestream can be very similar to a webinar, minus the hook and the sales pitch. There are great live streams out there by UXers but they are not the best option to build your network because engagement is usually focussed around the presenter.

IN SUMMARY

Networking can feel awkward for everyone and that's ok. Just stay present, ask questions and focus on other people to spark their interest. Keep in mind that you're not networking for the number of connections but rather their quality. The people you meet and connect with now could reconnect with you down the line. You never know when a work-related connection could become a friend for life.

∞

1. Lou Adler via a LinkedIn survey in 2016; 3000 participants in management and staff roles. https://bit.ly/NetworkingSurveyLinkedin

PERSEVERE AND AVOID BURNOUT

I believe that as a growing designer you should invest as much extra time as possible to develop. This might sound like hustle culture, which is now linked to burnout, but that isn't what I mean.

I don't mean that you should work extremely hard until you break down. I want you to understand why we experience burnout in the first place, so that you can know how to prevent it while still putting in the work needed to get you where you want to be.

Ultimately if you want to excel at anything, you will need to work on the edge of burnout but without falling into it. To paraphrase clinical psychologist Jordan Peterson's lecture on success and perseverance: *successful people must go out and find their breaking point first. Then, when you know where and what your breaking point is, you can walk just beside it.*

Many people struggle to do this successfully. According to a Gallup report[1] 76% of employees in all industries experience burnout at least sometimes. The report also highlights that simply reducing work hours is not going to make much of a difference. I'd argue that's because reducing work hours doesn't address the root causes.

ROOT CAUSES

The root cause of burnout is usually working very hard for an extended amount of time to no avail. For example, you might commit to an exciting project, but then that project becomes challenging, stress piles up and you don't feel any benefit to doing it in the first place.

Furthermore, as you keep hammering, the work doesn't deescalate; you're forced to keep the same pace and intensity. It might feel like there's no end in sight or the end you can see is not rewarding. You feel deflated.

Based on the report, the underlying root causes can also be expressed in several components:

Lack of autonomy and support

Unfair treatment at work, a lack of support or unclear communication from your manager are some of the top reasons for burnout based on the Gallup report. All of these issues limit our natural potential to do the best work we can.

There has to be a good match, alignment and work distribution between the doer and the manager. You'll probably have managers who need to be involved in everything you do because they think they need to support you. In doing this, they limit your autonomy to the extent that you don't feel that your work is valued.

Lack of time to complete the tasks

The Gallup report acknowledges that we are resilient and can push for a long time before crossing the burnout line. However, we must also recognise that our situations are not ideal and everyone's burnout line is in a different place. The reality of our jobs is less than ideal.

I recognise that I can spend extra hours at work — at this stage in my life — but I'd never expect that from anyone on my team. What I do recommend is for you to know yourself and your limits. Work to the best of your ability within these limits.

Inappropriate level of challenge and growth

A challenge that's too big or too small can be equally detrimental to your growth. Both will stunt your performance and keep you at the same place you were yesterday. To progress your career appropriately you have to take on slightly bigger challenges over time but without them becoming unmanageable.

Lack of appropriate reward and recognition

While there's variance in what we see as reward and compensation, they matter to us all. The reward isn't necessarily monetary compensation or external perks but, more often than not, connects with intrinsic motivation, sense of achievement, recognition from peers and seniors as having contributed to a shared effort.

HOW TO PREDICT BURNOUT BEFORE IT'S TOO LATE

There's a lot of schools of thought when it comes to gauging the worthiness of a challenge, but I subscribe to the following framework to assess if you should keep going:

The winner's effect

I first discovered this concept in Ian Robertson's book of the same name. He covers the science of success, and some methodologies for how to become successful.

The primary premise is that in order to become successful, you should build up your challenges incrementally. For example, if you want to become a world-renowned public speaker but you have never done public speaking before, you should start by talking to a few friends. Then, depending on the outcomes, learn from it and take on a more significant challenge, such as speaking in a meet-up. Then, take an even more substantial challenge, and so on.

Many designers get burned out because they take on one challenge that's too big instead of growing gradually through smaller challenges to become ready.

Are you facing the dip or a cul-de-sac?

Initially an analogy in Seth Godin's book The Dip (a highly recommended read), this concept describes how everything worth pursuing in your life is going to be challenging and push you to the limit.

Every challenge will have the dip where the endeavour gets harder before either it gets easier or it never gets easier and becomes a cul-de-sac. So, if you are in the midst of a struggle, you should step back and be very honest with yourself: is this environment a short dip, or something you are stuck in as if running on a hamster wheel. If it's the latter, you'll most definitely burn out.

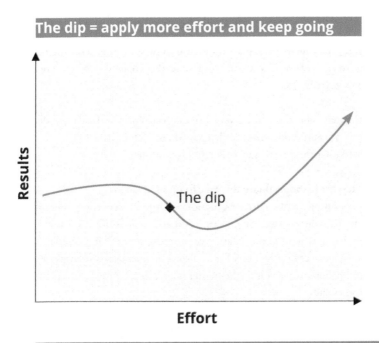

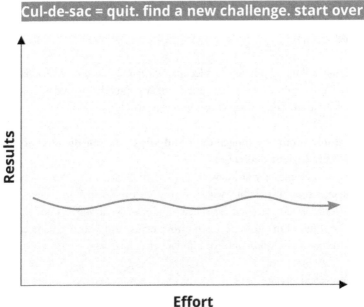

∞

BUT IF YOU FIND YOURSELF IN A PICKLE...

If you find yourself in a place where burnout seems to be on the horizon, and you're unsure if you can overcome the challenges, there are a few things you can do.

Ultimately, you need to be very honest and objective first to understand where you are and what challenges you're facing. The following tactics helped me through several challenging situations:

1. Step back and evaluate if it's a dip or a cul-de-sac

It's simple: is the current situation a naturally occurring, one-off challenge that you can overcome, learn from and benefit from? Or is it a dead-end that has a minimal chance of improvement? For example if after several unsuccessful requests for a raise your manager still hasn't created a plan for how to get you to the higher salary, then it might be time to look for a new job.

2. Outline the terms of perseverance and quitting

In other words, clearly define what you are willing and not willing to tolerate. If the going gets tough, define the specific criteria that would make you quit.

I'm not talking about minor hiccups or even significant challenges. No, what I'd like you to do is write a few bullet points that would describe the intolerable stuff that, if faced continuously, would burn you out.

3. Think about the longer term and what you can do to contribute given the current challenges

For example, if you know that it's a cul-de-sac and you must change course as soon as possible, what can you do to benefit from being in this cul-de-sac while you look for a new opportunity? If you're stuck in a fire pit of a job with no hope for improvements, can you use your current project for a case study until you find a better job?

In one challenging situation, I knew that I would need to hustle for a few months. Even though I was struggling mentally, I made the best of it by focussing on my portfolio. Knowing that I could turn the situation into a strong case study made it easier to live through, as it gave me a purpose.

4. Define your work-to-recuperation threshold and recovery intervals

If you're facing a potential burnout but none of the previous points helped you make a decision, perhaps the issue is that the cadence of your approach is off. I've seen many juniors who struggle because they can't adjust their natural pace to that of a business, department, project or immediate design team.

Some people are made to be nimble, fast and genuinely agile; others need time to process things, and that's alright. While these things change over time, it would also be worth outlining the ideal cycles of recovery and work sprints. Don't forget that UX is a marathon of small but intense sprints.

5. Talk to other people

Even if you don't identify as an introvert, chances are that you don't communicate your frustrations outwardly. Rants on social media don't count – they are actually what contributes to the very same problem of isolation and lack of real social support. It's essential to connect with other people who can listen and give you a different perspective on things.

I already covered why and how you should use the existing communities or local events. Those are the unwritten support groups that can make all the difference, especially at the beginning of your career in UX.

6. Never make hasty decisions. If you feel like giving up, sleep on it first instead of reacting to the urge.

Remember that things worth pursuing will always have challenges and dips, and sometimes what seems like the end of the world is something that your future self will laugh at. Be proactive, objective and very honest with yourself, but never reactive.

In terms of burnout, every person will have limits that, when crossed, cause burnout. But the fear of burnout shouldn't stop you from facing obstacles and difficulties. Just take them on incrementally to prevent burnout.

If you walk away from this chapter with a single takeaway, let it be this: **find and define your burnout limits, then take your efforts a notch down from there and continuously perform at that capacity.**

---

1. *Employee Burnout: Causes and Cures.* Gallup Report from 2020: https://bit.ly/GallupBurnout

AFTERWORD

I hope you have found this book useful. While I've tried to include as much meaningful and actionable advice as possible, in the editing process I had to remove 2 whole chapters and trim down an additional 10% of the book. This book took approximately 800-1000 hours to write, over a period of around 2 calendar years of daily writing. The range is wide because I lost count of how many times I had to sit down and work on it anew.

I could have written an even bigger book. An almanack of everything UX. Some of my earlier drafts were headed that way, however, as I wrote them I realised that you don't need more complexity in your already challenging life. Grasping UX and getting into the field is already a hard nut to crack, so why make it tougher?

Writing a book is also hard to crack. I had second thoughts and considered pulling the plug on this project several times. For example, I feared that some of my advice might not be applicable to many because it has been a decade or more since I broke into the industry myself. Just like I described in the book, I had to face my own internal and external blockers to finish this effort.

To get through the doubts, I'd remember all the praise and positive feedback I got from people who benefitted from my portfolio reviews, my advice on peripheral tools, and other tactics to get into the industry.

More importantly, what I realised is that almost none of those tools and methods matter if you don't cover the fundamentals of what UX is. It is understanding and doing true UX that separates those who get into the industry from those who struggle. If you get these fundamentals right, then the rest such as great project work, case studies and other evidence takes care of itself.

You still need to sweat those details in order to be competitive enough so that hiring managers see potential in you, however you have to grasp the underlying methodology first. My call to action for you is simple: revisit the basics of UX every once in a while so you don't steer away from what truly matters.

The whole process of writing this book has been very similar to what the typical UX process is like: frame the problems, understand the user, ideate and prototype the ideas into writing. By reading this book, you are effectively user testing my work. This is exactly why I'd like to hear your thoughts, news of your success and other feedback.

I feel like the worst thing for any book is to collect dust after it's been purchased. I'd like you to USE this book as an actionable guide: highlight stuff, mark the pages you want to come back to, write your thoughts in the margins, rip pages out if necessary and stick them where you can see them all the time, discuss the book with other people and pull it apart, do whatever you want with it just as long as you USE it.

∞

THANK YOU FOR READING
THIS BOOK

I really appreciate the interest that made you pick this book up.

If you found it useful, please leave a review on a platform of your choice. Additionally, if you know someone who is considering a career in UX or is struggling to get a UX job, share this book with them.

Don't stop there though, **if you enjoyed it make sure to connect with me** on the following channels:

VAEXPERIENCE on Youtube:
https://www.youtube.com/vaexperience

VAEXPERIENCE website::
https://vaexperience.com

Experience Designed newsletter:
https://vaexperience.com/Experience-Designed

The Design Squad UX community on Discord:
https://bit.ly/DesignSquadDiscord

For other versions of the book please visit: https://bit.ly/GetIntoUX

Don't forget to check for the downloadable content mentioned in a few different chapters: https://bit.ly/GetIntoUXContent

I really appreciate all of your feedback, and I love hearing what you have to say. I also welcome your input to make the next iteration of this book and my future books better.

Many thanks,
V / A

ACKNOWLEDGMENTS

In no particular order: graphic designer Jonas Perez Studio for the 1st edition cover. Editors: H.P., D. Alsamsam, Robert Night Jr., who all provided brutally honest, candid and constructive feedback. Wife and better half Helena, who has always been supportive of me spending hundreds of hours working on this book, as well as plenty of other projects. Family. My former and current design peers, design teams and its individual members. Also, my former mentees who taught me more through me mentoring them, than I could have done on my own. Some of their stories are also retold in *the real stories of designers* chapter. Private book beta team that provided candid feedback early on, directly and indirectly contributing to making this book what it is today: Michelle Pinsky, Kamil Faryna, Jamie Ryan, Tina Singh, Dr. Sukriti Sharma, Hali Sanderlin. Business and marketing advisors: S. Hooti, K. L., O. Omoniyi. All the mentors in my life: great bosses, teachers, professors, peers, juniors, challengers and frenemies and many more. Furthermore, my several *mentors by proxy* who's ideas and quotes I've used throughout this book. VAEXPERIENCE Youtube channel audience that engages with questions and keeps me producing educational content. The Design Squad UX community and people helping each other with actionable advice.

Everyone else who directly and indirectly participated in this experience. You know who you are. Thank you.

ABOUT THE AUTHOR

Vy (Vytautas) Alechnavicius is a experience design leader, an award-winning user experience and user research team manager, and a design educator to many.

Over the past decade, Vy has been involved in a variety of projects and companies, including: Tesco, SONY, GOV.UK, Arriva, Currys, Shell, HCA Healthcare, BP, KPMG, among many others. Vy has established and grown small-to-large experience design and research teams, mentored and up-skilled UX designers of all specialties, and helped shape design communities.

On a typical day, you'll find him in his office working on the next project. These days his focus is on giving back to the wider experience design community.

Reach out and connect on the following channels:

twitter.com/va_experience

instagram.com/vaexperience

youtube.com/vaexperience

linkedin.com/in/vaexperience

REFERENCES AND BIBLIOGRAPHY

Macintyre, Tadhg. (2014). Will the real winner please stand up? A review of The Winner Effect: The Neuroscience of success and failure by Ian H. Robertson 2012.

Robertson H. Ian, 2012: Winner Effect: The Neuroscience of success and failure. Bloomsbury Publishing; 1st edition (7 Jun. 2012)

What Mentorship really means - Simon Sinek, Facebook video: https://www.facebook.com/simonsinek/videos/what-mentorship-really-means/2647721008880920/

The Richness of Inner Experience: Relating Styles of Daydreaming to Creative Processes; Claire M. Zedelius* and Jonathan W. Schooler, Department of Psychological and Brain Sciences, University of California, Santa Barbara, Santa Barbara, CA, USA https://www.ncbi.nlm.nih.gov/pmc/articles/PMC4735674/

Placebo Effects of Marketing Actions: Consumer May Get What they Pay For; *Journal of Marketing Research*, 2005: https://stanford.io/3Eg8ryA

Effects of a Cognitive Intervention Package on the Free-Throw Performance of Varsity Basketball Players during Practice and Competition;

Dwight W. Kearns, Jane Crossman, Lakehead University; Issue published: December 1, 1992
https://journals.sagepub.com/doi/abs/10.2466/pms.1992.75.3f.1243

"The Disciplines of UX" by Dan Saffer (2008)

W.K. Kellogg Foundation Evaluation Handbook (1998): https://www.aacu.org/sites/default/files/LogicModel.pdf

Willink, J., & Babin, L. (2015). Extreme Ownership. St Martin's Press.

Voss Chris (2016). Never split the difference: negotiating as if your life depended on it. New York : HarperBusiness, an imprint of HarperCollins Publishers

The business value of design. McKinsey & Company 2008; https://www.mckinsey.com/business-functions/mckinsey-design/our-insights/the-business-value-of-design#

Don Norman, Why I Don't Believe in Empathic Design, 2019. Adobe ideas: https://xd.adobe.com/ideas/perspectives/leadership-insights/why-i-dont-believe-in-empathic-design-don-norman/

Dessart, Laurence & Pitardi, Valentina. (2019). How stories generate consumer engagement: An exploratory study. Journal of Business Research. 104. 10.1016/j.jbusres.2019.06.045.

Altutcher James. Choose Yourself: Be Happy, Make Millions, Live the Dream: CreateSpace Independent Publishing Platform; 5.1.2013 edition (June 3, 2013)

Ferriss Timothy, The 4-Hour Chef: Amazon Publishing (20 Nov. 2012)

Nassim Nicholas Taleb (2012). Antifragile: Things That Gain from Disorder. Random House.
NNG / Chris Roher's Landscape of UX research methods, 2014: https://bit.ly/UXRmethods

Eric Jorgenson (2020). The Almanack of Naval Ravikant: A Guide to Wealth and Happiness. Magrathea Publishing.

Taleb, Nassim Nicholas (2018). Skin in the Game: Hidden Asymmetries in Daily Life. Random House.

Original Twitter thread by Jenny Theolin (Design director and strategist): https://twitter.com/JennyTheolin/status/1293816514060193792

Risk sensitivity as an evolutionary adaptation; Arend Hintze, Randal S. Olson, Christoph Adami & Ralph Hertwig, 2015: https://www.nature.com/articles/srep08242

Storytelling as Adaptive Collective Sensemaking; Lucas M. Bietti, Ottilie Tilston, Adrian Bangerter, 2017. Topics in Cognitive Science published by Wiley Periodicals, Inc. on behalf of Cognitive Science Society

Daniel Engelberg, 2021 Linkedin: https://www.linkedin.com/posts/daniel-engelberg_uxdesign-changemanagement-activity-6833392913729236992-YAA0

Atomic Habits, Clear, James, Published: New York : Avery, an imprint of Penguin Random House, (2018)

James Altucher, The 1% Rule for Creating All, 2018 Medium: Habitshttps://medium.com/the-mission/the-1-rule-for-creating-all-habits-67a53553d284

Minto, Barbara. 2002. The pyramid principle: logic in writing and think-ing. London: Financial Times Prentice Hall.

SCQA framework and Minto's pyramid of storytelling by Barbara Minto: http://www.barbaraminto.com/

Kate Aronowitz 2018 Medium. Who sets your priorities?. https://medium.com/@katearonowitz/who-sets-your-priorities-6283910549c0

Reiter, What Got You Here Won't Get You There: How Successful People Become Even More Successful. New York, NY: Hyperion, 2007. Goldsmith, Marshall., and Mark Reiter.

"Eleven lessons. A study of the design process" (PDF). Design Council. Retrieved 6 April 2021.

Möller, Ola (9 January 2015). "The Double Diamond". MethodKit Stories. Retrieved 3 September 2019.

"What is the framework for innovation? Design Council's evolved Double Diamond". Design Council. Retrieved 6 April 2021.

Gallup Report, 2020 - "Employee Burnout: Causes and Cures" https://www.gallup.com/workplace/282659/employee-burnout-perspective-paper.aspx

Stanford Marshmallow test. Simply Psychology: https://www.simplypsychology.org/marshmallow-test.html

Tim Brown. Design Thinking. Harvard Business Review, June 2008

Kelley, D. and Kelley, T. (2015) Creative Confidence: Unleashing the creative potential within us all. Harper Collins, USA

Lou Adler via Linked in survey in 2016; 3000 participants in management and staff roles. https://www.linkedin.com/pulse/new-survey-reveals-85-all-jobs-filled-via-networking-lou-adler/

Value hierarchies across cultures, Shalom H.Schwartz, Anat Bardi, 2001: https://journals.sagepub.com/doi/abs/10.1177/0022022101032003002

Why you only need to test with 5 users by Jacob Nielsen, 2000: https://www.nngroup.com/articles/why-you-only-need-to-test-with-5-users/

Gladwell, Malcolm, 1963- author. Outliers : the Story of Success. New York :Little, Brown and Company, 2008.

Garrett, J. J. (2010). The elements of user experience (2nd ed.). New Riders Publishing.

10 Usability Heuristics for User Interface Design. Jakob Nielsen. on Apr. 24, 1994; Updated Nov. 15, 2020. Also: https://www.nngroup.com/articles/ten-usability-heuristics

Knapp, Jake (2016). Sprint: How to solve big problems and test new ideas in just five days.

The spotlight effect in social judgment: an egocentric bias in estimates of the salience of one's own actions and appearance; T Gilovich 1, V H Medvec, K Savitsky, 2000: https://pubmed.ncbi.nlm.nih.gov/10707330/